The Continuing Story of Beatles Lyrics:

The History and Storytelling of 15 Beatles Tunes

The Continuing Story of Beatles Lyrics
The History and Storytelling of 15 Beatles Tunes

Kyra Droog

Ryan McMillen

With Austin Mardon & Catherine Mardon

GM
PRESS

First Printing: 2021

Cover Design and typeset by Clare Dalton

ISBN 978-1-77369-596-9

Golden Meteorite Press

103 11919 82 St NW

Edmonton, AB T5B 2W3

www.goldenmeteoritepress.com

Preface: by Catherine Mardon

Music is meaning.

People inherently connect to music because they are able to connect the lyrics and music within songs to specific aspects of their own lives. A song about a breakup will speak to someone who has just gone through a breakup. A love song will speak to a couple who has just gotten engaged. A song about a car will speak to someone who has always imagined themselves driving a hot rod. Regardless of the original intention of the song, or the reason the song was written, people connect to music because they are able to see themselves and their stories within the songs that they listen to. This makes music particularly meaningful; after all, once we connect a moment or a memory to a song, we keep those associations for the rest of our lives. We remember what music was playing when we broke up with our significant other. We remember what played when we slow danced at our prom. We remember the first song at our wedding. These songs will cause us to feel specific ways when we listen to them, regardless of what the singer intended when we hear the song; we take these songs and internalize them, giving them unique, personal meaning.

Music is connection.

Think about the last time you attended a concert. Chances are, you were packed in with at least a thousand other people that were there for the same reason as you: to experience the music of your chosen band, live and in-person. The anticipation as you wait for the band to appear onstage is palpable: everyone around you is chattering with excitement. When the band enters to the dramatic tunes of their first song, they are met with a wave of energy as every single person in the stadium leaps to their feet shouting and cheering. As the concert continues, the crowd sings along, waves candles and flashlights for the slow songs, and shrieks in excitement throughout the high-energy songs. For the duration of the concert, every single person in the stadium is connected: packed shoulder to shoulder, singing along at the top of their lungs, and sharing a magical musical experience.

Music is storytelling.

Songs aren't often written just for fun, or just because a tune happened to pop into a musician's head in the middle of the night. Songwriting and composition is much like the writing of a story: it takes time, effort, and a huge amount of thought and consideration. With so few words to work with, and a reasonably short song duration, the choice of instrumentation, tempo, and tone take an important function within songs. Every aspect of a song tells a story. In fact, songs are stories: they share a moment, a feeling, or a tale for listeners to experience and enjoy. Though the concept of storytelling is typically relegated to physical pieces of storytelling, like this book, it's a firm fact that storytelling exists in many different dimensions: oral stories, music with and without words, plays, television, and more. Music is one of the strongest methods of storytelling because it combines words and stories with music that pulls at our heartstrings and encourages us to feel, often in the same ways as the singer or the character in the singer's story.

Music is universal.

Music is one of the most meaningful methods of storytelling, because it is able to be understood across languages, cultures, and other barriers. Music without lyrics still tells specific stories and makes people feel in specific ways, regardless if they know the story behind the song in advance of listening to it. Music brings people together, because when people listen to music, they share experiences. They share emotions. They share a connection unlike any other. People refer to music as a universal language, a concept which will be explored in this book, and say that it makes them feel close to each other, particularly as they experience the music live. Music transcends typical boundaries, encouraging connection even in the darkest times in history. Music provides hope and strength to those who need it. When we are happy, sad, or even just need a mood boost, we sing. When our voices sing together, we feel powerful: we are powerful. Music gives us an outlet to express ourselves, no matter where we came from, what colour our skin is, or what God we believe in. Music truly is universal.

Beatles music is unprecedented, in all categories.

When the Beatles first got together, they were just four kids from Liverpool looking to share their music with the world. As we look back on those moments, we realize that those four lads represented so much more than just music: the Beatles brought about a music and cultural revolution within the 1960s. They spoke, intentionally and unintentionally, about a variety of hot-button topics through their music. The Beatles toured the world, sharing their live music with hundreds of thousands of fans across the globe - creating connections through music. They told incredible stories; of young children leaving home, of nonsensical submarines, and of love, heartbreak, and misery. Their songs are a staple in any musical education, and for good reason. the Beatles brought the world together through music.

This book provides a deep dive into a wide variety of Beatles tunes and Beatles stories, but first, provides some necessary context so that we can completely understand these tunes and stories that we explore. It begins by providing a definition of music, and a variety of music fundamentals that are explored within the Beatles songs. Then, it explores the concept of music as a language, and provides a definitive response to the question: is music actually a universal language? From there, the book takes us through the 1960s and the Beatles story so that we have a firm understanding of what social, cultural, and societal factors influenced the creation of the Beatles, and what was happening within the world as the Beatles began their rise to fame. Finally, the book explores the backgrounds and stories of 15 Beatles tunes: some of their most popular songs, and some songs we haven't heard in years. Beatles music is so incredibly popular and has so many stories and ideas: the value of exploring these stories and understanding the context behind them is nigh unexplainable. By taking the time to understand the stories behind these songs, we are able to better understand the motivations of the Fab Four, and enjoy their music on an even deeper level.

Introduction: Music and Storytelling

Before we can begin to explore the many stories that the Beatles shared with us, we must first take some time to understand the art form within which the Beatles created: music. By considering some of the main storytelling methods within the musical medium, we will be better equipped to analyze and consider the effectiveness of specific stories within the Beatles discography. With this in mind, it's time to delve into music, and the many ways stories can be told through this art form - and not just through lyrics.

Defining Music

It may seem like a simple task, to define the term 'music,' since it is such a large and important part of our lives. Music plays in the background while we are in the shopping mall. Music plays during our workout sessions, to help keep us motivated. Music is in the background and foreground of each movie or TV series we watch. We listen to music to help us feel: depending on our mood, we listen to music that will make us happier, music that will motivate us, or music that will remind us of a special moment in our past. No two people are going to listen to a song and think about the exact same thing, because both intentionally and unintentionally, we connect with music based on the lives we have lived. When we consider music in this way, it becomes clearer just how difficult it can be to define music in a universal manner.

It makes sense, then, that hundreds of technical definitions have emerged from various musical scholars, all of which are different. Some definitions vary widely in terms of basis and fundamentality; other definitions are similar, but disagree in the more technical aspects. Our journey through music begins, then, by considering a few of these definitions and how they connect to us and our topic of discussion. Once we've taken this opportunity, we will open our minds to a greater understanding of the very basis of our topic: breaking down any pre-existing thoughts and feelingsand considering new ways of thinking about, talking about, and defining music.

Miriam Webster defines music thusly: "the science or art of ordering tones or sounds in succession, in combination, and in temporal relationships to produce a composition having unity and continuity" (Merriam-Webster, 2021). This definition of music is particularly technical: it references the basic aspects of sound that make up music (something we will delve into later in this chapter), and references the importance of creating relationships between tones to create sounds that have continuity and unity. This definition doesn't, however, consider some of the more modern musical tendencies that explore music that purposefully discontinues the concepts of unity and continuity in order to explore new musical territory. Does this mean that the definition is incorrect? Of course not - it just means that this definition is one view of what aspects make up the complicated concept that is music.

The Encyclopaedia Britannica refers to music as: "art concerned with combining vocal or instrumental sounds for beauty of form or emotional expression, usually according to cultural standards of rhythm, melody, and in most Western music, harmony" (Epperson, 2020). This definition is particularly interesting, because it refers to music solely as an art, and not as a science. It also specifies how the sounds that make up music are created, and how they are often categorized based on cultural standards. The fact that this definition notes cultural standards is important, as it recognizes that music can mean different things to different cultures. For example, the basis upon which music is composed and judged would be different in Canada than it would be in India, France, or Russia. Different parts of the world, and different cultures within, value aspects of music at different levels: for some, the most important aspect is the rhythm; for others, it is the melody and harmony. Denoting this distinction reminds us that no matter how we think about music, there is someone else that will consider it differently. In short, this definition not only explores the aspects that make up music but also the cultural values placed on those aspects, which reminds us that we need to consider how music is valued in order to properly define music.

The final definition of music we will consider is from the Cambridge Dictionary, which defines music as: "a pattern of sounds made by musical instruments, voices, or computers, or a combination of these, intended to give pleasure to people listening to it" (Cambridge Dictionary, 2021). This definition focuses on another aspect of music: the intent. By acknowledging that the intent of music is to bring pleasure to the people who hear it, this definition reminds us of the purpose of music: instead of exploring *how* music is created, it explores *why* music is created. With this consideration in mind, we remind ourselves that by this definition, any sounds created by a combination of voice, computers, and instruments can be considered music so long as its intent is to bring people pleasure. It's also interesting to note that this definition includes computers as creators of musical sounds, which opens up a new avenue of opportunity when establishing what fits within a definition of music.

So what definition then, dear reader, will we be using as we journey through this book and explore the very basis of what makes music, music? Instead of scouring the internet for an imperfect definition, we're going to take the best aspects of the three above definitions to create our own. For the purposes of this book music is an art form created with a single sound or a variety of sounds whose intent is to encourage feeling. All music, but the music we are exploring in particular, channels a specific emotion and, through a variety of aspects that we will soon explore, shares that emotion with listeners. From the haunting chants of the early medieval period to the grandest of symphonies to the sweetest of love songs, music, at its core, creates connection through feeling.

With this definition in our minds, it's time for us to move forward: first, to break down music into its most basic technical aspects and briefly consider each of them. This exploration will provide us with the technical knowledge and understanding to explore the concept of music as a language - and how it can cross all the boundaries that separate us as humans to touch our hearts with feeling. Then, we can jump into the next section, which will provide us with the cultural connotations and Beatles background that we'll need to have a full understanding and appreciation of the Beatles songs we will then explore.

Music Fundamentals

In order to truly be able to understand and recognize specific nuances within music - Beatles music in this case - there are certain musical terms and concepts that we need to identify and explore. Later in this book, we will be delving deeply into music, not only in terms of the lyrics and their meaning, but also in terms of the ways in which songs are built musically. By exploring these musical building blocks, we will be giving ourselves the tools and knowledge to take apart the pieces that make up these incredibly well-known tunes and understand the logic behind the ways in which they were built. This in turn will allow us to consider not only the superficial surface of the songs, but also the deeper intent, and the ways in which we are impacted by the song. These tools will also provide us the knowledge and opportunity to explore any type of music we please: we can take this knowledge that we're putting specifically towards Beatles books in this context and utilize it freely in our everyday lives in our own preferred music genres. One of the most beautiful things about music is that it relates to everyone universally, but also individually, and being able to explain some of the universal appeal is a true and exciting gift.

Rhythm

When breaking music down into its most basic aspects, the logical place to begin is with rhythm. Rhythm is one of those concepts that everyone thinks they understand, but in reality, lots of people think rhythm is one thing when it's actually a term with lots of other definitions falling underneath it. Edith Sitwell, a well-known poet and music critic, says that "rhythm might be described as, to the world of sound, what light is to the world of sight. It shapes and gives new meaning" (Sitwell, cited in Kerman & Tomlinson, 2015). Rhythm is the real base of music, creating a measurable way to understand music.

So what is rhythm? Interestingly, much like the definition of music, the definition of rhythm as regards music has also been highly contested. As Peter Crossley-Holland explains:

> Attempts to define rhythm in music have produced much disagreement, partly because rhythm has often been identified with one or more of its constituent, but not wholly separate, elements, such as accent, metre, and tempo. As in the closely related subjects of verse and metre, opinions differ widely, at least among poets and linguists, on the nature and movement of rhythm (2020).

It's important for us to understand, then, that rhythm is a blanket term: a term that has different aspects that fall technically beneath it. We're going to define a rhythm as "the actual arrangement of durations - long and short notes - in a particular elody or some other musical passage" (Kerman & Tomlinson, 2015, p. 4). This definition acknowledges rhythm's tendency to be a blanket term, as it is the arrangement of notes - a smaller building block - to create music. Instead of defining notes, we're now going to consider how we measure notes: using beats.

As Kerman & Tomlinson note in their book *Listen*, "beats provide the basic unit of measurement for time in music; if ordinary clock time is measured in seconds, musical time is measured in beats" (2015, p. 4). To help us really understand the impact of beats, let's consider the way in which they are used in workout music by thinking about the tempo, or the speed, of the music. When we want to go for a run, we listen to music that has a certain number of beats per minute (bpm) to keep our energy at a high level. If we want to match the beat of a song with our footfalls as we run, we are even more specific about the bpm, since it will then have a direct impact on our running speed. When we are doing yoga or stretching after a workout, we don't want to listen to music with a heavy beat - we want music that flows more freely to help us relax. The beat of a music is not only an integral piece of building a song; it's also an important part of how the song is classified and the energy that the song carries with it.

Beats are then organized into meter, or "a strong/weak pattern repeated again and again" (Kerman & Tomlinson, 2015, p. 5). When we think of meter, we think of a conductor waving their baton to count the beat - one, two, three, four/ one, two, three, four - for the musicians in the orchestra. This pattern of four beats is called a measure, or a bar. In some cases, there can be six beats in a measure, in some cases four, and in some cases three. There are many options available to musicians when they begin to build a measure: how many beats, and where they put the emphasis in the meter are two important aspects.

Let's consider the emphasis on a specific beat within a measure and see how impactful the emphasis can be. If we recite a measure with four beats, we have four options for emphasis:

One, two, three, four

One, *two*, three, four

One, two, *three*, four

One, two, three, *four*

If you read those in your head, or aloud, the emphasis shifts slightly with each line. Though the emphasis may not sound important when considering this example, as we get into our analysis of these Beatles songs, you will begin to understand how the change in emphasis can have a deeply profound impact on the music that we listen to.

It's important to remember that rhythm and the associated aspects of music are fundamental to our ability to break down songs and understand what specific musical techniques cause them to be effective, and how that effectiveness can be measured. As we move forth in our understanding of music fundamentals, we have to keep rhythm in mind, as it will always be the basic building block from which we base our analysis of songs.

Tone

Tone isn't a single musical idea: it actually encompasses a wide variety of concepts that are integral to our understanding of the building blocks of music. To begin our conversation on tone, we are actually going to initiate discussion on a seemingly unrelated topic - pitch. The Encyclopaedia Britannica defines pitch as the "position of a single sound in the complete range of sound. Sounds are higher or lower in pitch according to the frequency of vibration of the sound waves producing them" (2019). Different instruments, of course, have different pitches: a flute is considered a high-pitch instrument, whereas a trombone is considered a low-pitch instrument. Now, we need to remember that at its most basic, sound exists in waves. The pitch of an instrument, then, relates to the way in which the instrument creates sound waves. For example, a bell creates sound waves differently than the strings of a violin, which creates sound waves differently than a flute. We don't need to understand the complex nature of the science of sound here, but what we need to keep in mind is the way that sound is created in relation to an instrument.

Pitch also relates to dynamics or loudness and softness, when it comes to music. Dynamics are noted in music to help musicians understand how loud or quiet they should be playing in relation to their colleagues. Let's think about an orchestra for a second. If every instrument in an orchestra played at the exact same level of loudness, there are some instruments that you would hear over others, as they are naturally louder than others. Imagine playing a flute next to a trumpet: without question, the trumpet would drown out the flute if they were being played at the same dynamic. If the music called for a flute solo, however, the music would be written so that the trumpets and other instruments would play more quietly, and the flute would play louder, to ensure balance within the orchestra. The common musical dynamics are as follows:

Pianissimo - *pp* - very soft

Piano - *p* - soft

Mezzo Piano - *mp* - medium soft

Mezzo Forte - *mf* - medium loud

Forte - *f* - loud

Fortissimo - *ff* - very loud

Of course, there are many ways that composers can inform musicians of their dynamic, including asking them to move from quiet to loud and loud to quiet at a variety of speeds, but for the purposes of this book, understanding the different musical dynamics at their most basic is what we need. It is, however, important to note that the feel of a single note can change depending on if it's played loudly or quietly. Consider a clarinet: a single, quiet, wavering note from a clarinet might feel sad and lonesome, but a loud and purposeful note might feel shocking or energizing. This, of course, is in part determined by the pitch of an instrument, but leads us into another fascinating concept: timbre, or tone colour.

Tone colour, or timbre, is defined as "the characteristic that allows us to distinguish the sound of one instrument from another. Every instrument produces its own tone color. For example, when you hear a clarinet and a guitar play the exact same pitch, the tone color of each instrument allows you to tell the difference between the sounds that you hear" (Coughlin, 2018). The concept is, of course, much more complicated than this simple note, but we have included it here so that when we talk about the history of instruments and the importance of specific instruments within specific songs, we have an understanding of why the difference in instrumentation is notable. Think of it this way: you know the difference between a Lennon-sung song and a McCartney-sung song because of the tone colour of their voices.

With our newfound understanding of tone, we can now better study the techniques that the Beatles used in their songs, and how tone and related musical concepts factor into their songs and the perceived meaning of their songs. We aren't quite done with our music fundamentals exploration though - it's time for us to dive into the concept of melody, which will help us better understand some of the ways in which the Beatles tell their stories within their songs.

Melody

The concept of melody will have a huge impact on our discussions later on in this book, as we discuss the difference between melodies and harmonies, countermelodies, motives, and much more. Since the Beatles are so well known for their glorious harmonies and sweet melodies, this is a good time at which to explore the most basic ideas behind harmonies, melodies, and more, so when we delve into the songs themselves, we will be able to understand just how impactful these concepts are to Beatles songs.

Let's begin by remembering how the Encyclopaedia Britannica defines pitch: "the position of a single sound in the complete range of sound. Sounds are higher or lower in pitch according to the frequency of vibration of the sound waves producing them" (2019). A melody is, in fact, "an organized series of pitches" (Kerman & Tomlinson, 2015, p. 24). The Encyclopaedia Britannica explains further, saying that melody is "the aesthetic product of a given succession of pitches in musical time, implying rhythmically ordered movement from pitch to pitch" (2021). The melody line, then, is the line that's most prominent within a specific song. Let's explore this idea using a well-known song, and one that the Beatles covered in their early days: "My Bonnie."

As you'll remember, the first lyrics to "My Bonnie" go like this: "My Bonnie lies over the ocean/My Bonnie lies over the sea." Take a moment and hum or sing the first line. You'll notice that as you hum each word, or each note, the pitch changes. The note you hum for "my" is lower than the note that you hum for "Bonnie," and when you hum "Bonnie," you split the word into two phrases: 'Bon/nie' where the first half is higher than the second half. In essence, the notes leap from low to high and then continue down in a step-like fashion. The notes that you are humming, in that order, constitute the melody line for this song. This is the same for any other song you would choose, whether the song has lyrics or not.

"My Bonnie" is considered a tune: "a simple, easily singable, catchy melody such as a folk song, a Christmas carol, or many popular songs" (Kerman & Tomlinson, 2015, p. 25).

The term melody includes tunes, amongst other types of recognizable pieces of music like motives and themes. Motives, for lack of a more complicated explanation, are melodies fragments that are returned to at certain points in the song. Think about, for example, the Imperial March from the Star Wars films. The motive for that song is the strong "dun/dun/dun/*dun*/dun/dun/*dun*/dun/dun." This motive returns time and time again; sometimes in the foreground of the song, and sometimes subtly in the background. The theme of the Imperial March, then, consists of this motif played over and over again in different pitches, with different instruments, and with different intensity levels. Themes and motives exist in songs with lyrics as well: think about the chorus that exists in pop songs, and certain riffs within other songs. The iconic guitar riff in "Blackbird" for example, is a motif, which then becomes a theme throughout the song.

Harmony, then, is playing notes of different pitches that sound pleasing together at the same time. Think about the Beatles song "If I Fell." The part that goes "If I gave my heart to you/I must be sure from the very start/that you would love me more than her" is predominantly harmonized, where John and Paul are singing the same words with different notes that sound beautiful together. the Beatles are well known for their incredible harmonies, and "If I Fell" is quite possibly one of the best examples of their masterful harmonic work. As you would expect, though, harmony is more complicated than its basic definition. To help us better understand harmony, we're going to explore two related concepts that are particularly important in our exploration of these popular Beatles storytelling tunes: consonance and dissonance.

"If I Fell" is a perfect example of consonance. The notes that are played together within "If I Fell" are beautiful: they feel comfortable to us as we listen, and make us smile and wonder in amazement how Lennon and McCartney manage to weave such beautiful melodies and harmonies. In musical terms, consonance is "the impression of stability and repose experienced by a listener when certain combinations of notes or tones are sounded together" (Encyclopaedia Britannica,2021). The notes in "If I Fell" feel stable: they feel like they intrinsically belong together. This feeling, this concept, is the idea of consonance. Dissonance, on the other hand, is "the impression of tension or clash experienced by a listener when certain combinations of notes or tones are sounded together" (Encyclopaedia Britannica, 2021). This is an intentional clashing of notes that makes the listener feel uncomfortable; as if something is wrong. The feeling is correct - listening to two notes played together that aren't consonant is an uncomfortable sound that can be utilized in a variety of ways within a song to add tension and other emotion. Kerman & Tomlinson explain this concept well:

> A dissonant chord leaves a feeling of expectation: it seems to demand a consonant chord following it to complete the gesture and to make the music come to a point of stability. This is called resolution: the dissonance is said to be resolved. Without dissonance, music would be bland: like food without salt or spices (2015, p. 29).

Melody, harmony, consonance, and dissonance, all play big and important parts in the music we listen to on a daily basis, but particularly in the Beatles music that we are about to explore. Now that we have a foundational knowledge of these terms and how they are used, we can continue our exploration of music fundamentals with our final section: instrumentation.

Instrumentation

As we are about to learn, instrumentation plays a massive part in the ways in which we connect to and understand songs. We will take a deep dive into the ways in which historical connections to instruments have a meaningful and often unnoticed impact on the way we consider music played by specific instruments in a later section, but now, it's time for us to delve into the main instruments that the Beatles favoured - both in their early days and after they became a studio band. By exploring the background of these instruments and some of the things we unknowingly associate the instruments with, we will better be able to understand just why the Beatles - with their guitar, bass, drums, and vocals, captured the world in the way that they did. With that in mind, let's consider the most popular instrument in early Beatles music: the guitar.

Now, there are four types of guitars we are going to explore in this section, as each of them has a distinct sound and a particular use. Before we get into specific types of guitars, though, let's take a few moments and consider the history of the guitar itself, and what we tend to associate with the concept and sound of a guitar. Interestingly, as with many early instruments, the exact history of the guitar isn't confirmed - but there are theories as to when and where the first guitar-like instrument made its appearance. It is important to note that this history is not intended to be comprehensive in any way, but is instead intended to be a brief historical introduction to stringed instruments that paved the way to the creation of the modern-day guitar.

The popular theory is that the term 'guitar' originated from the Greek term 'kithara' or 'cithara.' The kithara was "an ancient Greek stringed instrument similar to but larger than the lyre and having a box-shaped resonator" (Merriam-Webster, 2021). Likely, this was the earliest version of the modern-day guitar. Interestingly, the mythology surrounding the advent of the kithara is mixed: in some cases, Hermes is attributed to its creation, but there are also many stories of Apollo playing the kithara, as well as many images of him holding the kithara. Regardless of its mythological invention, for our purposes, the kithara will be the earliest version of a guitar, as far as history has made us aware.

The kithara made way, then, to the lute, which was another precursor to the modern-day guitar. The Encyclopaedia Britannica defines a member of the lute family as "any plucked or bowed chordophone whose strings are parallel to its belly, or soundboard, and run along a distinct neck or pole. In this sense, instruments such as the Indian sitar are classified as lutes. The violin and Indonesian rebab are bowed lutes, and the Japanese samisen and the Western guitar are plucked lutes" (2021). For the purposes of this book, a lute (distinct from a member of the lute family) is a string instrument from the Renaissance and Baroque musical eras that was particularly popular in Europe. Its design changed course over the years, as the makers of the instrument began to improve its functionality, but in general, it looked much like a modern-day guitar, as it included a slim neck with a hollow round belly with a hole cut in the middle. Strings were then strung over the belly and onto the neck, and the instrument was played by either plucking the strings or in some cases using a plectrum - the historical equivalent of a guitar pick.

It's important to understand that there are hundreds of instruments throughout history that could have been a precursor to the guitar, and that it would be impossible and illogical to list them all here. Instead, what we need to take from the above section is that the actual origins of the guitar are unknown, but the most recognizable piece of guitar history from the Western world is the lute. There are hundreds of instruments that vary slightly from the lute and kithara throughout history, and there is a likelihood that those are all connected in some way to the modern day guitar, but proving those connections is something that historians are still working on, as they tie instruments to time periods, to specific music, and to other instruments that pre- and post-date them.

We mentioned that there are four types of modern guitars that we are going to explore, and it's time for us to jump into that exploration. While these instruments are similar, it will help us as we move through our exploration of Beatles songs to understand the purpose of these different guitars, as they each provide a different purpose within a song. By understanding these purposes in action, we will be able to add another layer to our understanding of the storytelling within Beatles songs, and why certain songs make us feel certain ways even before we hear the lyrics.

Now, guitars are a particularly fascinating subject to discuss, because in many cases, lots of the differences between guitars (like the acoustic and classical) are slight and nuanced, yet still seem to make all the difference in the world. In general, there are four main aspects that differ between types of guitars, and these are the four aspects that we will explore in relation to the four guitars we are considering. These four main aspects are: shape and size, strings, feel and suitability, and sound production. We'll begin our discussion by taking a look at the difference in shapes and sizes between our four guitars.

As we learned in the earlier section, guitars typically take on a similar shape: a wide body, rounded shoulders, and long neck. That said, even though there is a general shape for guitars, there are a wide number of variations from the general shape that account for some of the differences between types of guitars. Whereas classical guitars typically stay the same shape - the 'usual' guitar shape - acoustic guitars have a variety of shapes and sizes. Acoustic guitars vary in terms of the size of the guitar itself, the thickness or thinness of the body. The variations offer different types and volumes of sound; in general, the bigger the guitar, the louder the guitar. Electric guitars are different from acoustic and classical guitars because of their shape and makeup. Instead of being hollow instruments, electric and bass guitars are substantially thinner than acoustic and classical guitars; this difference relates to their sound production, which we will discuss later on in this section. Between our four types of guitars, electric and bass guitars have the most variation in terms of shape and size: "since the size and shape of the body of the electric guitar tend not to influence the sound of the instrument as much as classical and acoustic guitars, manufacturers are free to play around with different designs." (Ze, n.d.).

Now it's time to talk about guitar strings. One of the most obvious differences between guitars, outside of their size, shape, and sound, is the number and type of strings the guitar uses. The materials that guitar strings are made of play into which guitars said strings can be used on. For example, it's common to use nylon strings on classical guitars, but those same strings shouldn't be used on acoustic guitars because of the light bracing on acoustic guitars. Instead, acoustic guitars typically use steel strings that are coated with either brass or bronze. As Mason Hoberg explains, "as a general rule, brass strings are always going to be brighter than bronze strings" (Hoberg, 2017), which means that the same guitar can make a different sound based on the type of strings it has.

Electric guitar strings are often steel strings with or without nickel plating; the nickel strings offer richer sound than strings without the additional plating.

The number of strings is also important to consider when it comes to guitars, as they change between types. Bass guitars typically have four strings, but can feature any number of strings - having five and six strings on a bass guitar is becoming more and more common. Acoustic and classical guitars usually have six strings; each string having a different thickness to assist in the creation of a different type of sound. Electric guitars also typically have six strings, however, there are other configurations to consider, including any number of strings between six and twelve. It isn't difficult to understand that the difference in number of strings absolutely impacts the type of sounds that guitars are able to produce; however, there are nearly an innumerable amount of options when it comes to the types of guitars, when considering the body and string combinations.

Feel and suitability are notoriously difficult to describe; much like wands in Harry Potter, the guitar has a part in choosing its human. There are a variety of factors within the category of feel and suitability that impact a person's decision as to which guitar they would prefer. Between the type of strings and how they feel while a person is playing; the size of the neck and the fretboard; and the size, shape, and weight of a guitar and how it feels while a person is sitting, standing, and playing, the feel and suitability of guitars are reasonably individual. That said, there are, of course, reasons outside of feel and suitability for which a person would choose a specific type of guitar - it is just important to consider how a guitar feels for a musician before they begin their journey of playing on that instrument.

The biggest differences in sound productions are between the hollow body guitars and the flat guitars. The hollow body guitars produce sound through the vibrations of the strings. "When a string is plucked its vibration is transmitted from the bridge, resonating throughout the top of the guitar. It is also transmitted to the side and back of the instrument, resonating through the air in the body, finally producing sound from the sound hole" (Yamahaw, 2021). Electric and bass guitars produce sound differently, as they don't have the hollow body through which to resonate sound. "[The bass guitar] produces sound when its metal bass strings vibrate over one or more magnetic pickups (although non-magnetic pickups are occasionally used as well). The pickups then transmit a signal, via instrument cable, into an amplifier, which allows the bass to be heard at a wide range of volumes" (Masterclass, 2020). In essence, then, the biggest difference is whether the guitar requires amplification - bass and electric guitars - or not - acoustic and classical guitars.

Guitars are truly fascinating instruments, and they differ dramatically in their makeup and sound based on their design. It would take books upon books to explore the unique and specific different types of guitars in all their glory, so we have provided you here with a brief overview to help you understand the differences between the types of guitars. Since guitars were, in the early stages of the Beatles' career, their main instruments, the understanding we've gained here will assist us greatly within the second and third sections of our book as we explore the ways in which specific songs make us feel and why those songs make us feel that way.

Music as a Language

Music has been around since the very beginning of human history, and as we just discussed, is an integral part of our lives. Regardless of where we grew up, what language we speak, or what colour our skin is, we all have a deep and rich musical history: a musical history that connects us to our ancestors, allows us to feel when we need to, and helps us navigate our day-to-day lives. That said, different parts of the world and different cultural groups have very different types of music entrenched in their histories, which means that the musical market is flooded with a wide variety of types of music. With that kind of variety, you're basically guaranteed to find something you'll connect with, right? Well, that statement might actually be more correct than you would think.

There exists a longstanding theory that music is a universal language; that it transcends typical linguistic boundaries to create deep and meaningful connections between individuals, regardless of their background, language, or knowledge. Since the focus of this book is on music and storytelling, it seems natural for us to discuss this concept of musical universality and the ways in which this concept supports storytelling in music outside of the simplicity of lyrics. There are two distinct ways to tackle this topic, and we will be making a brief dive into both: considering music as a language in linguistic terms, and considering the aspects and history of music that makes it universal. By doing so, we will be arming ourselves with intrinsic knowledge that supports our understanding of music as we move forth to discuss the ways in which the music of the Beatles connected countries, generations, and people together in harmony.

There is much debate about whether or not music is technically a language when it comes to considering music in relation to linguistic rules. To be completely fair to the topic, this means that we should explore both the positive and negative arguments in relation to music being a language, which will thereby provide us with a full understanding of the debate at hand. First, let's take a brief look at linguistics itself and what the technical requirements are for a language according to linguistic rules. This exploration will provide us with the basis upon which to discuss whether or not music is a language.

According to the Linguistic Society of America, linguistics is "in a nutshell, the scientific study of language. Linguists apply the scientific method to conduct formal studies of speech sounds, grammatical structures, and meaning across the world's 6,000+ languages" (2021). In order to discuss linguistics, in this case, we must first define what constitutes a language. For the purposes of this book, we will use David Crystal's definition from the Encyclopaedia Britannica. According to David, language is "a system of conventional spoken, manual (signed), or written symbols by means of which human beings, as members of a social group and participants in its culture, express themselves. The functions of language include communication, the expression of identity, play, imaginative expression, and emotional release" (2021). Let's break that definition down into some talking points, which will outline our discussion regarding music and language. First, we'll consider whether or not music constitutes a system of conventional spoken, manual, or written symbols. Then, we'll discuss the ways in which music is used for human expression. Finally, we'll delve into some of the ways in which music does, or does not, act in the aforementioned functions of language. This exploration will then inform our decision as to whether or not music technically counts as a language, in linguistic terms.

To begin, let's explore music's tendency towards a system of conventional spoken, manual, or written symbols. As you are likely aware, ever since the first days of music, written forms of music have existed, along with music notes, to inform musicians of how they were expected to sing or play songs. It's expected that before that, much like a substantial portion of early history, songs were passed down verbally from generation to generation. When considering music's written symbols, it is clear that much like a language, these symbols have universal references. There are multiple methods of writing out musical notation, and to demonstrate their universality, let's explore a few of them.

Typical Western staff notation is the method of musical notation that you, reader, are likely most familiar with. This notation is dependent upon a 5-line bar, upon which musical notes, and other information for the musician, is placed. The time signature, placement of notes, and inclusion of clefs all provide essential information for the musician to ensure they are able to play the music in the way that the composer intended. Let's take a moment and compare typical Western staff notation to the English language. The musical notes themselves are equal to the words that we would typically write. The type of note - whole note, half note, sixteenth note, etc. - declares how the note is to be played, or how the word is to be read. Like an explanation detailing whether a character is saying a phrase while smiling or crying, types of notes and notation regarding the speed and intensity they are to be played with has a large impact on the emotion that a note or string of notes has in a particular piece of music. Of course, it would take an entire book to go into detail and discuss each of the individual notations and their impacts, but for this purpose, all we really need to understand is the way in which Western staff notation allows for a multitude of information to be provided from the composer to the musician, dictating parts of their performance much like a writer dictates the way a reader understands a specific concept or connects to a certain character.

Of course, there are also other ways to express musical notation, some that have existed for thousands of years. Oral traditions of music relied on solmization, or "the naming of each degree of a basic scale with a word or syllable" (Encyclopaedia Britannica, 2021). Different languages have different methods of achieving solmization, but the most recognizable in the Western world is do-re-me-fa-so-la-ti-do. This allowed discussion about musical phrases to be understood, as there was a connection between the note, its scale, and the way it is written on paper. Numeral notations, existing predominantly in Japanese and Arabic traditions, see the allotment of specific numbers to pitches; instead of using words or syllables, they used numbers to refer to aspects of a scale. There are also graphic ways of drawing out musical notation that don't include the typical scale seen in Western staff notation. For example:

> The Vedic chant of southern India uses a form of accentual notation: a dot beneath or above a syllable of text indicates a lower or upper reciting pitch. Analogous systems, involving dots and dashes, formed a notation for ancient Jewish cantillation and early Syrian Christian chanting. A more developed form

("ecphonetic" notation) was used for recitation of Byzantine liturgical chants (Encyclopaedia Britannica, 2021).

Finally, there are methods of noting music based on the way in which an instrument is played: seen most often for string instruments like guitars. This notation demonstrates the way in which the fingers are to be placed on the instrument in order for a musician to play a specific note. Though fairly uncommon for lengthy pieces of music, this can be an easy way for novice musicians to begin to learn to read music and remember their fingerings at the same time. Regardless of the ways in which music is notated, however, even with this brief overview we have proved that music is expressed in written and verbal ways through a series of symbols that have universal meeting to those who use that specific form of musical notation.

Now it's time for us to tackle the next concept in our discussion of music: the ways in which it is used for human expression. It is important for us to tackle the ways in which music is influential in our lives, which will lead into further discussion of historical significance and cultural associations in the next section. To begin our discussion, let's think about the prevalence of music in our lives. For many people, music is playing for a significant portion of their days, but until we actively think about it, that music can seemingly fall to the background since we are so used to hearing it. For example, think about your last trip to the mall. There is typically background music playing in the hallways of the mall, and different music playing in each store you enter. That said, you listen to music of some kind from the time you enter the mall to the time you leave. Then, chances are you listen to the radio or your favourite driving playlist as you drive home from the mall, and then maybe have a CD or the radio playing upon your arrival home. We listen to music while we work out, while we work, while we study, while we cook, and sometimes even listen to music to help us drift off to sleep. That's a lot of music!

That said, all of that music we listen to is selected with a purpose. When we work out, we listen to music that will provide us with the right energy for our workout - if we're stretching, we listen to soft music, but if we're pumping iron or running a marathon, we're going to queue up songs with a heavy beat, inspirational lyrics, and songs that keep us feeling energized and excited to achieve our fitness goals. If we're studying, we may listen to instrumental music; something to drown out any background noise and to help us focus without getting distracted by lyrics. And that's just when we are selecting music for ourselves. Stores that play music do so with an agenda: they want you to stay in the store, to feel a specific way while you're in the store, and to feel motivated to purchase something before you leave. This is one reason that extensive research has been completed on the ways in which music impacts people emotionally, and how that can be used to benefit individuals and corporations. Let's review some of that research so we can be clear on the ways in which music has been proven to express and evoke emotion.

First, we'll cover our bases and look at a study that proves the connection between music and emotion. In a 2016 study, researchers studied the impact of listening to sad music and familiar, happier music on individuals across Finland and the United Kingdom. The study found that "memorable experiences linked with sad music typically occurred in relation to extremely familiar music, caused intense and pleasurable experiences, which were accompanied by physiological reactions and positive mood changes in about a third of the participants" (Eerola & Peltola, 2016). The study focused on the way in which music could be used as a type of mood regulation for individuals: how listening to sad music can be sad but also cathartic, and how listening to happy, familiar, high-energy music can actually improve your mood. According to the lead author of the study:

> Previous research in music psychology and film studies has emphasised the puzzling pleasure that people experience when engaging with tragic art. However, there are people who absolutely hate sad-sounding music and avoid listening to it. In our research, we wanted to investigate this wide spectrum of experiences that people have with sad music, and find reasons for both listening to

and avoiding that kind of music. The results help us to pinpoint the ways people regulate their mood with the help of music, as well as how music rehabilitation and music therapy might tap into these processes of comfort, relief, and enjoyment. The findings also have implications for understanding the paradoxical nature of enjoyment of negative emotions within the arts and fiction (Eerola, quoted in Durham University News, 2016).

There are, of course, dozens of studies across the years that have proven the physical, mental, and physiological connection between music and emotion, which is yet another reason that we refer to music as a language. This study is particularly interesting, because where the focus is usually on how music can improve our mood, the focus here is on why we either choose to listen to or avoid listening to sad music, and the implications of that music on our emotions. Later in this book, when we talk about the Beatles song "Misery," we will consult another one of these theories which looks at the ingredients required to make a 'feel-good' song using what the author of the study dubbed the Feel Good Index. Studies like these agree with what we feel when we listen to music: we feel the strong connections that it provides us, and often feel as though we can connect specifically to the lyrics, the tune, or the artist, leading us to meld music and language together as one.

A 2012 study by Yuna Ferguson and Kennon Sheldon proved that listening to upbeat and positive music can, over a period of time, facilitate a more positive mood in an individual. This study had participants listen to either a more positive piece of music or a more negative piece of music a certain number of times over the course of two weeks. The study "showed that participants assigned to try to boost their mood while listening to 12 min of music reported higher positive mood compared to participants who simply listened to music without attempting to alter mood" (Ferguson & Sheldon, 2012).

Even the individuals who weren't attempting to alter their mood reported having higher levels of positive moods at the end of the study, resulting in the authors proving that "listening to positive music may be an effective way to improve happiness, particularly when it is combined with an intention to become happier" (Ferguson & Sheldon, 2012).

These studies prove without question that listening to music has an impact on human emotion and expression: physiological responses to music such as increased energy and positivity or feeling sad and crying all lead us towards the irrefutable conclusion that music and emotion are intertwined. The final study that we will consider focuses even more deeply on music's impact on us as individuals, and explores the ways in which music can have a lasting positive impact on our brain; in particular, our ability to recall specific memories once we become old. Before we dive into that study though, let's take a moment and remind ourselves of just how much is going on in our brains each day, and how we store memories with specific associations.

Our brains are constantly at work, from before we are born to after we die. Without our prompting, our brain reminds our heart to pump blood through our bodies, our lungs to suck in and push out air so we can breathe, and a myriad of other actions. We don't have to actively think about moving our bodies when we are reaching for a glass of water or furiously type away at a keyboard: our brain fills in the blanks and helps us function on an everyday basis. Even when we are using our brain, it's storing away memories all the time: the faces of our family and friends, whether or not we like the taste of bananas, and exactly how many steps we can walk in the dark before we run face first into our bedroom or bathroom door. If we remembered every single thing that we encountered, said, and did each day, we wouldn't be able to function because our brain would be so packed full of useless memories, thoughts, and focuses. This is another special wonder of our brain: without us knowing, it is able to filter out the unimportant information and keep a specific record of the information we need to know. Many of us have our credit card numbers memorized for online transactions. We remember our birthdays, social insurance numbers, and, of course, that embarrassing thing that we did when we were young - the one that our families are never going to let us live down.

Our brain holds so much information, but sometimes, that information can be difficult for us to pull to the forefront of our minds. A group of researchers at Dartmouth College proved that "the brain's auditory cortex, the part that handles information from your ears, holds on to musical memories" (Dartmouth College, 2005). This means that when we're listening to music, the memories that we associate with that music are stored as well. That's why when we hear the song that was playing during a proposal or a breakup or even during that one really good day at the bookstore, we have a seemingly sudden flashback to that moment: because our brain is remembering not only the song, but also the moments that we associate with that song. This concept has been used by researchers in musical therapy to help patients with brain diseases like dementia and alzhymers to help their memories: by associating a memory with music, the memory becomes stronger, and by cueing them to remember a memory that they already associate with music, they are able to remember the memory more clearly.

We could spend hundreds of books pouring over the studies of music and emotion, music and the brain, and music and language and still not even cover half of the studies that exist. For the purpose of this book, and for our discussion on the prevalence of music as a language, these aforementioned studies provide us with the context that we require in order to understand how music connects to emotion, and on an even deeper and more physical level, how music impacts the brain and our ability to recall specific memory or time. What we have done here, is satisfied our discussion around the ways in which music is used for human expression: through memory and emotion. Now, it's time for us to delve into our final topic in this aspect of our discussion: how music acts in functions of language.

The functions of language listed in our definition of language include: communication, the expression of identity, play, imaginative expression, and emotional release. Through our exploration in the previous section, we have explored ways in which music communicates emotion, and ways in which music provides emotional release; instead of focusing on these aspects of music and language, let's take a deep dive into one of the remaining three functions, allowing us to prove that music fulfills at least three out of five functions of language. It's time, reader, for us to explore the connection between music, language, and imaginative expression.

To discuss this topic, we're going to explore a 2017 study by Simone Ritter and Sam Fergus. These researchers were curious about the impact of music on creativity - a form of imaginative expression. To explore this topic, Ritter & Fergus prepared a study based on the concepts of divergent and convergent thinking. According to Jill Suttie, "modern science suggests that we all have the cognitive capacity to come up with original ideas— something researchers call "divergent thinking." And we can all select from a series of ideas the one most likely to be successful, which researchers call "convergent thinking"" (Suttie, 2017). Ritter & Fergus explored whether individuals listening to happy music or individuals listening to silence demonstrated greater divergent or convergent thinking after a certain amount of time. Their study found that "listening to 'happy music' (i.e., classical music that elicits positive mood and is high on arousal), as compared to a silence control condition, is associated with an increase in divergent thinking, but not convergent creativity" (Ritter & Fergus, 2017).

This study produced some groundbreaking results, because it proves that listening to happy music assists in divergent thinking, or coming up with original ideas. To an even greater benefit to our analysis of music, language, and imaginative expression, the music that Ritter & Fergus used was classical music: music without words, but that was dubbed as 'happy' music because of specific musical aspects within the songs. This study, therefore, proves the connection between music, language, and imaginative expression: listening to classical music that is universally understood as happy music creates an increase in imaginative expression, when compared to an individual that listened to silence. What does this mean for us? This means, then, that we have successfully proved that music fulfills at least three out of the five functions of language listed in our definition of language, and thus allows us to prove that music is a form of language.

In conclusion, let's review our findings. David Crystal defined language as: "a system of conventional spoken, manual (signed), or written symbols by means of which human beings, as members of a social group and participants in its culture, express themselves. The functions of language include communication, the expression of identity, play, imaginative expression, and emotional release" (2021). Through exploration, we found that music exists in various conventional written symbols, and that we use music to express ourselves as creators, listeners, and performers. We then explored three of the functions of language listed above, and proved their connection to music. It is only logical, then, that we take a moment to recognize that the oft-mentioned phrase "music is a universal language" is truthful: music is a language that transcends traditional barriers and brings people together. We'll end this section with a quote from Dr. Francis Winspear, who sums up music's ability as a language best:

> As a form of communication, music can transcend the boundaries of culture, differences in educational and economic backgrounds and barriers between nations. As such, music can help build harmony between people of all ages, races, cultures and beliefs in our own growing city" (Dr. Francis G. Winspear, quoted from the Winspear Centre website, n.d.).

Conclusion

In order to have a whole and complete understanding of the Beatles songs we are going to explore in this book, it is critical for us to understand some basic musical concepts so that we can go deeper than surface level in our exploration. This section has provided us with a surface level of detail about musical concepts - with the knowledge that there will be so much for us to explore in the future. As we move forward into our next section, which provides context to the time period in which the Beatles entered and fundamentally changed the music scene, this musical knowledge will stick with us, and assist us in our deep and meaningful exploration of the songs we know and love from the biggest band of all time.

Section 1: Setting the Scene

Introduction

The best way to truly understand the Beatles and the impact they had on the 1960s is to understand what society looked like within the 1960s. The 1960s were a particularly fascinating decade in history, and to best be able to understand the ways in which the Beatles songs we are about to discuss impacted society, we have to first take the time to know what that society looked like and how it was shaped by the Beatles. With this understanding, we will then be able to move forward and look at our 15 Beatles tunes - and in doing so, connect our newfound knowledge of the 1960s and the music that the Beatles released throughout the 1960s, leading us to a deeper understanding of exactly why the Beatles are known as the band that changed the world.

The 1960s

Cultural Understandings

The 1960's were a time of transition. The 1950's post-war era focused on rebuilding countries and societies. In the United States, there was a push to focus on families and careers, and the creation of the American dream; with nearly half the country's population being made up of people under the age of 18, there was an exciting new energy abound (PBS, 2005). That energy was only intensified by the election of John F. Kennedy and the space race that captured the hearts and minds of Americans. However, the optimism that held the American hopes would wane as the sixties continued and questions regarding war and peace would evolve into movements across America. With Americans having plenty of disposable income and plenty of businesses eager to collect it, it was inevitable that consumerism would sweep the country. This was only accelerated by the introduction of television into the homes of millions of middle class Americans, which helped spur everything in popular culture further than ever before. Products were advertised to households who had the money to spend on entertainment and novelty goods.

In Europe there was a focus on rebuilding from the destruction of the war, with new trends and ideas being built alongside the repair. Some countries rose out of the destruction better than others, though in most cases, the swingin' sixties was a decade of economic growth. Consumerism was making its way into society as people began to make more money and thus needed something to spend it on (European Union, 2019). While the western, democratic nations of Europe were thriving in rebuilding and forming new cultures and societies stemming from their capitalist systems, countries in the Eastern Bloc were focused on their growth as well. As communist nations, their success was based on ideas entirely separate from those of their western counterparts. Their sole focus was on the growth of the nation as a whole, not on burgeoning, radical ideals propagated by the youth or on consumerism. Their focus on growing state economies and furthering their technological advancements, displayed by Soviet Russia's involvement in the space race, would keep them close on a global scale with their democratic counterparts. Though the communist nation in the East attempted to cut off most influences of the western world to their citizens, some things were able to sneak through. Namely the music of the time and with it the ideas that permeated the western youth.

No matter the country, it was undeniable that there was a whole new culture being brought about by the youth of the world. Young people began to look for something different. More young people began questioning past ideas and traditions as the world was rebuilding itself. European students were creating a movement of new ideas. In England many young people were being influenced by the blues and folk music coming out of America. This took form in English genres of music such as skiffle, which pulled from American blues and folk music written and performed by predominantly black musicians (Dewe, 1999). In many ways, music was a way for young people to have fun while engaging with ideas that they were curious about. Artists such as Bob Dylan wrote about subjects that gave people pause, and made them ask more questions about the world around them. The public zeitgeist was changing, and so too was popular culture. Even teens residing within the Eastern Bloc would become influenced by the bits and pieces of rock music that seeped through the cracks.

Youth movements were also beginning to influence everything from fashion to politics. As the decade continued on, the youth movements would shift to more of a focus on peace and love following the violent assassinations of John F. Kennedy and Martin Luther King as well as the brutal and unforgiving Vietnam War. As the ideals and promises of America began to fade, students throughout the country would begin to ask harder questions and hold mass public protests. As young people around the globe began a movement of counter-culture, the music they listened to would propel those messages even further. Artists of all mediums began writing about the woes of the time, asking the leaders of their worlds more difficult questions through their works. In turn, people started doing the same as growing youth movements and artistry to its most popular extent would continue to influence one another into the 1970s

The Music Industry

The music industry coming into the sixties was in a good place. The American industry had created some huge stars such as Frank Sinatra, Elvis Presley, and Buddy Holly in the fifties along with the rise of Motown records. However, the young audiences the record labels were catering to craved something new. That is where folk music and rock music came in. Folk musicians like Bob Dylan wrote songs that were not only fun to listen to, but were written about societal issues at the time. Rock music on the other hand brought in the feeling of rebellion that young adults and teenagers shared at the time. With the desire for a fresh new rock sound, it was only a matter of time before someone set the stage for exactly that. What no one may have expected at the time however, is that new sound and energy would come from England.

England throughout the fifties had seen musicians become stars within their own country such as skiffle artist Lonnie Donegan. Where English artists hit a stumbling block was in the transition to the music scene in America. Whether it was a cultural disconnect or a matter of inopportune timing, musicians from England had an incredibly difficult time becoming popular across the Atlantic Ocean, let alone becoming stars. It wasn't until well into the sixties that England saw their own hit groups become international superstars. Bands such as the Beatles and the Rolling Stones would bring a sound to America that sounded fresh, one that was inspired by American rock and blues music but also had a distinct energy behind it. Their energy permeated through the masses as the music coming out of England traveled across the globe. By the mid-sixties these groups began accompanying their fresh and energetic sounds with lyrics that touched on issues at the time, just as folk musicians such as Bob Dylan had begun doing earlier in the decade. Whether it be protests against tax laws or an ode to the effective use of psychedelics, musicians were beginning to speak about subjects that people around the world, especially young people, were growing curious about.

The Beatles

The Beatles Story

On the surface it may seem like a simple fairytale story: four working class Liverpool kids go on to defy the odds and become one of the biggest bands in the world. However, there is much more to the Beatles history than that. What fans began to see in 1963 was the culmination of an exorbitant amount of hours playing music together in all kinds of clubs throughout the United Kingdom and Germany. Not to mention that the inclusion of Ringo Starr within the Beatles did not happen until 1962 when he replaced original drummer Pete Best, and that Paul McCartney was not the original bassist for the group: that honour belongs to Stuart

Sutcliffe. Before we get too far ahead of ourselves, let's refocus on their beginning: skiffle.

Skiffle music is a form of Jazz, Blues, and folk combined and played primarily on improvised or non-formal instruments such as jugs, washboards, and more. While skiffle may not be popular today, it was one of the most popular forms of music in England during the 1950's amongst young people. The emergence of skiffle, and particularly Lonnie Donegan's records, inspired many young English people to pick up whatever they could and start skiffle bands of their own (Dewe, 1999, p. 1). Two of these youths were John Lennon and Paul McCartney. In fact, before their first meeting John had already started a skiffle group called The Quarrymen. The two's first fateful meeting would come after Paul watched The Quarrymen play live. Paul, when recounting the event in the 1995 the Beatles Anthology series, said

> "There was a wagon and on the back of this was a little stage or something on this stage it was a few lads around and there was one particular guy I noticed at the front and in sort of checked shirt sort of blondish color hair little bit curly sideboards looking pretty cool and he was playing so that one of these guitars guaranteed not to crack you know not a very good one but but he was making a very good job of it you know I remember being quite impressed and he was doing a song by the Del-Vikings called 'Come Go With Me' and the thing about it was he obviously didn't know the words but he was pulling in lyrics from blues songs so instead of going 'come little darlin come and go with me' which is right he'd then go 'down, down, down to the penitentiary' he'd be doing some of the stuff he'd heard on Big Bill Broonzy records and stuff so I thought that's clever, he's pretty good" (McCartney, quoted in Smeaton & Wonfor, 1995).

After listening to Paul play guitar, John would soon convince Paul to join the Quarrymen after deciding that Paul was a better guitar player than those who were already in the group. It didn't take long for Paul to help recruit his grammar school friend and fellow guitar player George Harrison to the group. The next step for the group was to find a bassist, which was a position eventually filled by Stuart Sutcliffe, a talented artist friend of John's from the Liverpool College of Art. In fact, Paul and John convinced Sutcliffe to sell his paintings and use the money to purchase a bass guitar.

The group started playing small shows around England, but primarily in Liverpool. During this time is when the group changed their name from The Quarrymen to The Silver Beatles, also known by some variations such as Long John and the Silver Beatles. There are a few different stories on how they came up with the name. One account from the group is that they chose it as an homage to Buddy Holly's group The Crickets. Another account from Paul says that they took the name from a gang in the film *Wild Ones* starring Marlon Brando (Roberts, 2011, p. 14). Another notable about their name is the change in spelling of the insect beetles into Beatles. The change of the name creates a pun as a beat is a unit of measure in music or could be a reference to beatnik culture and beat rock n' roll music. During this time, it does not appear that the group had a permanent drummer playing with them, often playing with whoever was available for a show. Their search for a drummer to play consistently with the group didn't come until they were offered 15 pounds per month to play nightclubs in Hamburg. It was then that The Silver Beatles approached Pete Best, a drummer that had played with them before, to join them in Germany. Best agreed and the group of Liverpool lads sent off for their adventure in Hamburg in August of 1960 (Lewisohn, 2013, p. 341).

It was at some point during their German excursion that the Beatles dropped the silver from their name, as they played deep into the night in the St. Pauli district of Hamburg, a part of the city known for its breadth of entertainment. Those looking for an honestly good time and those who wanted something more depraved would both be able to find their fix in St. Pauli. At the time of their arrival in Hamburg, they were all incredibly young. The youngest of them, George, was only 17 years old and thus had lied about his age in order to get his passport (Lewisohn, 2013, p. 342). Their time in the nightclubs of St. Pauli was that of young people living recklessly while honing their trade. Often playing grueling, demanding sets late into the night throughout the week and especially on weekends, the boys needed to adapt quickly to their new schedule as the longest sets they played in Liverpool had been two hours, while now they were playing up to six hour sets on the weekends. Being natural performers, they learned very quickly how to interact and play with the crowd to get the reactions they desired.

> "The German audience liked the group's rough sound and their tough-guy act. John would insult the crowd and do crazy things like giving the outlawed Nazi salute. They would joke between sets and interact with the audience. Bruno Koschmider, the club owner, encouraged them to *mach schau* – 'Make show.' Their wild performances were good for business" (Roberts, 2011).

It was also in Hamburg where the group met three art students: Klaus Voorman, Jurgen Vollmer, and Astrid Kirchherr. Astrid is the most famous of the group when it comes to her connection with the Beatles as she took the now famous photos of them, often clad in their leather jackets and standing in shadows. She also took on a relationship with Stuart, who was already thinking of leaving the band. Their adventures in St. Pauli wouldn't last much longer however, as Harrison would be deported in December after it was found out that he was actually seventeen, and he wasn't the only one that would be deported. Soon after, Paul and Pete were arrested after they decided to play a prank on the club they worked for right before they took their services to another club in St. Pauli. The two were also sent back to England. John would follow after having his request to stay denied, while Stuart would stay in Germany with Astrid until mid-January of 1961.

Once back in Liverpool they took their time before returning to the stage, but once they did, they started to see success. Their new look and attitude cultivated in the hard to do bars of St. Pauli was something that Liverpool crowds hadn't seen before. With their leather jackets and cowboy boots, they had incorporated the image of a true rock n' roll band. One of the

Beatles first concerts upon return was at Litherland Town Hall at the end of December where they had one of Pete's friends replace Stu on bass, since he was still in Germany.

As the group played more shows they began to become more popular. Playing in venues such as The Casbah Coffee club, which was owned by Pete Best's mother, as well as a spot where the Beatles would make their name: The Cavern. With their stature in the Liverpool scene growing, the group decided to return to Hamburg for a short spell only months after most of the group had been deported. It was here that Stuart decided to leave the band and where McCartney took up the mantle as the bassist, much to Paul's chagrin. Here they would play more music for their fans in St. Pauli while also having their first chance at recording some music. By the beginning of July they had returned to Liverpool ready to make a statement in their hometown once again.

> "Kings before they left, they'd taken their performance to another, higher level: now a foursome, all in leather, even more dynamic, packing yet more punch and charisma, and bursting with the experience that only another 503 extraordinary hours on the Hamburg stage could have given them" (Lewisohn, 2013, p. 452).

The Beatles, now back in Liverpool, set off on showing their talent to the world: playing live shows throughout the summer in clubs around Liverpool, but most notably at The Cavern. By the time of September, things were going well for the group, but their growing popularity wasn't enough to keep John and Paul from boredom. The two decided to leave for Paris for a month, much to the dismay of the rest of the group and those surrounding them, and meet up with their friend Jurgen Vollmer. It was here that another transformation happened that would set the course for the Beatles image. John and Paul, impressed by Parisians attitude and style, decided they wanted to cut away the long, greasy rock star look that they adopted over the past year and incorporate a more clean style of cut that they would be known for in the coming years (Lewisohn, 2013, p. 487).

Upon John and Paul's return to Liverpool, the Beatles would continue to play shows around the area. It was at one of their shows in The Cavern where their destiny would be set in stone. At a show on November 9th, Brian Epstein came to watch the growing local sensation for himself. Epstein came from a line of entrepreneurs and at the time was employed as the manager of the record division in his father's record store. After hearing about the group from some of those who shopped at the department store, he decided to go see them for himself. What he saw impressed him.

> "They gave a captivating and honest show and they had very considerable magnetism. I loved their ad libs and I was fascinated by this, to me, new music with it's pounding bass beat and it's vast engulfing sound. There was quite clearly an excitement in the otherwise unpleasing dungeon which was quite removed from any formal entertainments provided at places like the Liverpool Empire or the London Palladium, though I learned later that the response to the Beatles was falling off a little in Liverpool -- they, like me, were becoming bored because they could see no great progress in their lives" (Epstein, 1964/2009).

After the show, Epstein approached the foursome and set up future meetings with them. In those future meetings he decided to make the jump and offer his services as the group's manager. Epstein travelled to London to pitch his new group of charismatic Liverpudlians to companies such as Decca and EMI, setting up further meetings and auditions for his group to impress and get signed. However, when that time came, the answer was less than what they were expecting. Both EMI and Decca didn't see in the Beatles what Epstein saw - a group destined for superstardom. Instead they saw them as just another rock n' roll band in a crowd of Elvis knock-offs. Dick Rowe, one of the top officials at Decca, famously told Epsteins that "groups of guitarists are on the way out" (Best 1985/2009).

It wasn't until Epstein found his way to George Martin, that the Beatles had a chance in the industry. Martin was a producer for the record label

Parlophone, a child company of EMI. Martin had not been a part of the process that rejected the Beatles after their EMI auditions earlier, and agreed to have the group audition for him. After the audition, the group went back to Liverpool and waited for the news. At the beginning of April John, Paul, and Pete flew to Germany to fulfill some gigs and George tagged along shortly after. However, the boys would receive more bad news before they heard anything good. Just as they landed, the three Beatles who had made the trip learned that their friend and former bassist Stuart had passed away by Astrid's side on April 10, 1962. George received the news back home in Liverpool. Still mourning the death of their friend, the Beatles pushed on through their misery and played their shows in Germany. All the while they were still waiting to hear from Brian regarding their recent audition with Parlaphone. On May 9th they finally received some great news in the form of a telegraph from Epstein: they were being offered a recording contract.

The Beatles returned to England in early June ready to record some material, including an original piece called "Love Me Do." While the recording session went fairly well, it was obvious to George Martin that there was still work to be done. While the charisma and the star power of Paul, John and to a lesser extent, George, was clearly evident, he had two main issues with the group. The first was that "Love Me Do" had some good points, he did not believe it to be a hit record, and based on what he heard, he wasn't sure that they had the ability to write a true hit. Secondly, and arguably more important, was the drumming ability of Pete Best. Best couldn't keep time with the rest of the group, causing the entire group to change tempo throughout the song seemingly every time it was played. It was here that George Martin decided that Best shouldn't be used in future sessions (Lewisohn, 2013, p. 645).

The group outside of Best had wallowed in the idea of kicking Best out of the group many times before, but now they were on the cusp of success and it was obvious more than ever before that they needed a fantastic drummer in the group. Discussions on who they would bring in were kept hush from Pete as the big three and Epstein worked to figure a replacement throughout the summer of 1962. Finally, the deed was left to Brian Epstein to commit, as he sat down with Best to tell him that he was being replaced by another drummer who was familiar to the group named Ringo Starr.

Ringo had been a prominent drummer in the Liverpool rock and roll scene for as long as the Beatles were around. His group at the time, Rory Storm and the Hurricanes, were a successful band in the area and had played in clubs in St. Pauli around the time of the Beatles German occupancy. Having always admired Ringo's ability from afar, the decision was made to bring him into the fold and cast Pete Best aside. the Beatles as the world would know them had formed. They were now a proper four piece in their own eyes, however some of their fans disagreed. There was pushback amongst their most hardcore fans for casting Pete aside, but that wasn't important to John, Paul, and George. All that mattered to them was to get better and become one of the biggest musical acts in the world.

The Beatles would continue to play shows in the area while also making television appearances. In September they made their way back into the studio with Ringo where they would record "Love Me Do," which would be their first record released with EMI. Though the record didn't have high hopes from those at EMI, Epstein did his best to get the Beatles and "Love Me Do" in front of people. It worked: "Love Me Do" made its way into the *NME* and the *Record Retailer* charts and prompted George Martin to bring the boys back in to record their next single, "Please Please Me" which reached number one on some record sale charts, though technically not the Beatles first number one single as it did not reach the peak of the official UK singles chart. The Beatles continued their success into the next spring, as they released their first LP *Please Please Me*, named after their second single, in March and their single "From Me To You" became their first song to reach number one on the official UK singles charts.

The *Please Please Me* album shot up to number one on sales charts and suddenly, Beatlemania had truly begun. Over the upcoming months the group would be featured prominently on British television programs while touring all over their island nation. Nearing the end of the year the four had already recorded and released their second LP of the year titled *With the Beatles*, which would unsurprisingly place them at the top of record selling charts in the UK once again. They were even asked to perform for the British Royal Family at the Royal Variety Performance show, where they showed off all the charm and wit that had won the hearts of so many already. The Beatles were also becoming a name in Europe as they had played shows in Scandinavia and France, everytime coming back to hysteria from Beatles fans welcoming them home.

However, there was still one huge question for the Beatles if they wanted to be the biggest band in the world - could they bring Beatlemania, at its current level, to America? The group was wary of their prospects in America as they had seen so many British stars fizzle when they played shows in the United States (Lewisohn, 2013). Of course, looking back we know that it most definitely did, but the place where those worries were answered was during their infamous performance on the *Ed Sullivan Show*. Sullivans first exposure of the group came in late October of 1963 when his flight was delayed in London by screaming Beatles fans welcoming them back from a Scandanavian tour (Stark, 2005, p. 22). Though he didn't know anything about their music, the fan-fared pandemonium he saw first had was enough to book the four Liverpool lads for his television program in 1964.

Although unsure of the success they would find in America, the band's worries would soon be dissipated once they landed in New York. The media, inquisitive of these young men from Liverpool, had the chance to interview them and found them likable and humorous just as the media in their own nation had. Of course, their performances on the *Ed Sullivan Show* in February of 1964 is what sent Beatlemania into the stratosphere. As their song "I Want To Hold Your Hand" was their first to reach the pinnacle spot on American charts in December of 1963. Unsurprisingly, their American fans were excited to see the group that had started to take over the radio waves live in their own country. During that first American tour, the Beatles, as well as those around them, began to realize that the reaction from fans was unlike anything they had ever seen before. It wasn't out of the ordinary to see the police escorts that followed the group on the brink of collapsing due to the pure pandemonium that the fans, who just wanted to see a Beatle let alone meet one, had created.

> "The Beatles were on stage for only 25 minutes. I'm not sure if this was because they were scared to death or if it was due to the fact that 25 minutes was about the limit of hysteria that any of us could handle. You could hear very little of the music above the screams. People would stay quiet just long enough to recognise the song -- was it 'Long Tall Sally' or 'She Loves You'? -- and the screaming would start again and remain for the rest of the song. And the flash bulbs never stopped going on-off, on-off" (Bedford, 1984/2009, p. 81).

By the summer of 1964, the Beatles had toured all across the world to countries including Australia, Holland, and Hong Kong. Their time touring included a North American stretch that had them playing thirty-two shows in thirty-four days across the continent (Stark, 2005, p. 152). But they weren't just busy with live performances: their album *A Hard Day's Night* was released in July of that year to a rabid fanbase who wanted even more music. It was also the first album from the group that contained no cover songs; instead, every song was a product of the now famous Lennon/ McCartney writing duo. *A Hard Day's Night* also coincided with a film of the same name. Both the album and the film became financial and critical successes as the album rose to the number one spot one charts all over the world, including a 14 week hold on the top spot in the American Billboard album chart: the film became one of the biggest films of the summer as it became a hit at the box office and with critics who were won over by the group's charm and wit.

Through to the end of the year, the group would release yet another album, *Beatles for Sale*, as well as continue their heavy touring schedule across the globe. Their popularity was at an all time high, with millions of fans around the globe buying any merchandise that had the four mop-headed men's faces on them. From clothing to collecting cards, they had merchandise on any product that had space to fit their image onto it. They were on top of the world, but that had its own downsides as well. Once everyone knew who they were it was difficult for the members of the band to keep anything out of the public eye. As the Beatles dealt with these issues along with their own personal troubles, their music would take a step in maturity and creativity as they made their way into 1965.

In December of 1965 the band released their album *Rubber Soul* to the world. The title of *Rubber Soul* was a play on "plastic soul" - a term used by black musicians to criticize the lack of heart or passion and derivative stylings of some of the British Invasions artists' music (Zolten, 2009). On the album, the group had begun to experiment with their sound by incorporating more interesting songwriting and instruments, such as the sitar, into their catalogue. This album was also the first to put pressure on the group, as it was the first where they didn't have previously written material to record for it. Over the course of three months John, Paul, George, and Ringo spent countless hours — at times days — writing and recording new tracks. *Rubber Soul* was also the first album they produced that was influenced by their use of drugs, specifically cannabis and acid. To fans of the Beatles the album has been cited as "the pot album" (Lewisohn, 2002/2009, p. 132). All of the hard work would pay off well for them, as it would make its way onto the top spot of many record charts in the world. 1966 continued their trend of constant touring with the rest of their time being taken up by writing and recording new material. That new material would come in the form of *Revolver*.

Revolver, released in August of 1966, was their most ambitious album yet. The group, having made their creative home in the recording studio at Abbey Road, pushed the limits of the technology available to them to create sounds that would change popular rock music forever. Tracks such as "Eleanor Rigby" with it's grandiose sound due to the production and inclusion of classical stringed instruments, and "Tomorrow Never Knows" which used looping effects to create an overwhelming wave of guitar sounds showed the world that the Beatles were not just a fun boy band anymore. It wasn't just in the album's production where that distinction could be made. The songwriting on *Revolver* further showed the groups continued maturity as the love songs that lead them to popularity were replaced with songs with themes outside of romance. Loneliness on "Eleanor Rigby" and the UK's tax system on "Taxman" proved that the group, while not above writing songs about love, were also focused on exploring subjects outside of the themes that helped make rock and roll popular in the first place.

While their tour continued into 1966, it began to take a toll on the Beatles' already strained lives. Many were going through issues in their own personal lives. Lennon was falling further into despair regarding his marriage, and would soon meet his future wife, Yoko Ono, in late 1966. Paul and George were also going through their own issues in regards to their engaged/married lives. Not only were they under pressure from all sides, but they were also becoming more focused on their songwriting and song creation. They wanted to explore their own creative capabilities in their albums, but their touring schedule was preventing this. By late August, shortly after the release of *Revolver*, they decided to stop touring and focus solely on the music they created due to the combination of extreme stress (which we will explore later on in this book) and drive to explore their own creative possibilities. Furthermore, not only did the group decide to stop touring but they also decided to take a break. Harrison made his first trip to India and Lennon moved further into the realm of film as he starred in the war movie *How I Won The War*. McCartney on the other hand was already thinking of their next project. When the four all reconvened, McCartney told the group of his idea that they should take on the role of a fictional band.

In late November the writing and recording of the next Beatles album would begin, with it releasing six months later in June. *Sgt. Pepper's Lonely Heart Club Band* very well may be one of the first concept albums in the realm of rock music. In it, the Beatles are replaced by a colourful group with facial hair who the world hadn't seen before. It was an idea that allowed the four who couldn't get away from their fans, the media or the expectations placed upon them to take up a new face and release the shackles to push their creativity, and audiences expectations, to the limit. The musical and lyrical ideas on this album were light and dreamy, while also being incredibly creative and at times psychedelic. While concept albums today often connect tracks together through an overarching theme or story, the concept of *Sgt. Pepper's* was the band itself and the freedom the titular band had in creating their songs. The album also helped elevate the ever-growing hippie movement, as well as the drugs that came with it. Perhaps it was because of this love and peace attitude that they, especially Harrison, were pulled toward spending time in India and learning from the teachings of Maharishi Mahesh Yogi.

> "Listening to this record was, as with the previous Beatle album, an experience unlike any other. These were not merely more sophisticated lyrics (again), more diverse themes (again), and a unique soundscape (again). Fans had learned to recognize and expect artistic development, but the way the entire album played with levels of reality was a whole new thing to ponder. It's the band they've 'known for all these years' -- or is it? And who is this Billy Shears? Where would this performance be taking place?" (Leonard, 2014, p. 143).

The Beatles dominance continued throughout the world. Even without touring they were still able to find their way into the minds and hearts of millions. They truly were on top of the world. However, that would all soon change and their worlds would come crashing down while there they heard the news that their long-time manager and close friend Brian Epstein passed away in late August at the age of 32. Shocked and heartbroken, the group pushed forward in their creative endeavours while trying to figure out the business side of the industry. After all, it was Brian who took care of the group's business and ensured that the group was operating at their absolute best. the Beatles had lost their #1 fan, or as some say, the fifth Beatle. With Epsteins passing, the beginning of the end had begun for the musical powerhouse from Liverpool. Each Beatle tried to cope in their own way. Lennon reached out to his father, Harrison continued his studies with Maharishi Mahesh Yogi and tried to get the group to embark on a journey to India to further advance their studies. Paul was unsure of this idea and instead pushed the other three to complete their next project: a film and soundtrack duo release off of the back of their last creative venture (Stark, 2005, p. 218-219). When *Magical Mystery Tour* was released in the winter months of 1967 the album was warmly received, while the film was anything but so. The film, which they aired on BBC1 on Boxing Day, was panned by Beatles fans and critics alike leaving the group in an even deeper state of vulnerability.

Though they may have had a dud film on their hands, they were still as popular as ever. But with everything they had been through in the past months, they decided to finally go through with the excursion to India that Harrison had been clamoring for. While there they would begin working on songs that would appear on their eponymous album that would release later in the year. There were also tumultuous times in some of their personal lives. Throughout 1968, Lennon would make his affair with Ono quite open with his current wife, who would divorce him by the end of 1968. McCartney would go through his own relationship woes as his fiance would call off their marriage in the summer of 1968, while Harrison and Starr would have their own ups and downs in their relationships due to their heavy psychedelic drug use and continuous infidelites.

They would finally release their next LP *The Beatles*, or more commonly known as the *White Album*, a year after *Magical Mystery Tour* was released. *The Beatles* was their most diverse album yet covering multiple genres over a runtime of over an hour and a half, which made it their longest project to date. While the album received much praise, it was during it's recording that the seams of the group truly began to tear apart. Each member had their own idea of the kind of musical direction they wanted to pursue. Paul for instance wanted to create catchy songs intertwined with lyrics that could easily connect with others while John was much more focused on writing songs that pushed boundaries and questioned current social and political ideas. This self-serving, never ending cycle put the group through more frustration than they were already experiencing.

The Beatles continued to work on projects such as the *Yellow Submarine* album that paired with an animated movie that featured the group. But each Beatle continued to fall apart from one, not only musically or regarding personal matters, but also in regards to how they should handle their business, or rather who should handle their business. 1969 proved to be a productive, yet somewhat destructive year. They would release *Abbey Road* months after *Yellow Submarine*, all to further commercial success. Meanwhile, the tensions were growing hotter behind the scenes, as the search for a new manager culminated in two individuals: Allen Klein and Lee Eastman. The two men had their own supporters within the band, with John, George, and Ringo backing Klein, while Paul pushed for Eastman (who would soon become his father-in-law). When the majority backing Klein decided to move ahead with him, McCartney would make his decision - he was through with the Beatles. Paul made his announcement that his time with the group was over on April 10 of 1970, and just like that the group had disbanded. The disbandment of the group was not a surprise to any of the Beatles, as Lennon had mentioned to his fellow bandmates and Klein that he was planning to leave the group as early as September of 1969 (Cott, 107, p. 2013). If anything the surprise was that Paul was the one to make it public knowledge. The group released their last album *Let It Be* a month after the news of Paul's departure made its way around the world. Some fans held onto hope that their favourite group would release another album one day, but this idea was put to bed by the often cutting interviews made by members of the band where they would openly criticize one another. The Beatles were finished, they were no longer on top of the music world, at least not together. However, their influence continues to live on in the hearts of many to this day.

The Beatles and Cultural Influence

Paul, John, George, and Ringo set off a cultural phenomenon that changed the world of music, celebrity, and fandom forever. Beatlemania took hold of everyone who listened – from fans to musicians. It would be difficult to find someone in the western world who has not heard of the Beatles, let alone heard their music. The songs they created can still be heard on major radio stations and commercials. Cover versions of those same songs feature in prominent films and television shows to this day. Merchandise donning their faces or logos can be widely purchased today. While Elvis Presley may have been one of the first musicians to reach immense levels of popularity and success, the Beatles may have been the first group to do so. One of the most fascinating aspects of Beatlemania was how each member had their own fans. Now, while John and Paul may have led the way as far as popularity, George and Ringo also had a sizable fandom of their own. This phenomenon is similar to what we see happen with boy bands today. In this sense, the Beatles may very well be the first boy band to draw international acclaim and fandom, leading the way for the entire music industry to try to replicate it to this day by assembling a group of handsome, talented young men.

Not only were they one of the world's first musical supergroups and a huge hit with fans, they were also a big hit with fellow musicians at the time. Groups such as the Beach Boys and the Rolling Stones were in friendly competition with the Beatles, attempting to write the next big hit song or record while vying for the top spot on charts around the globe. The group's innovative techniques with track recording, specifically how many tracks they recorded with and how they manipulated those tracks in post-production, were a huge influence for artists at the time. The mind bending sounds that the Beatles produced became the sounds of partying, of drugs, and of revolution. Famously, after Brian Wilson of the Beach Boys listened to the Beatles *Rubber Soul* album and thought every song on the record was near perfect. It was the influence of this record that fueled his creativity into producing one of the biggest rock albums of all time in the Beach Boys *Pet Sounds* (James, 2020). After *Pet Sounds* the Beatles would come back with *Sgt. Pepper's Lonely Hearts Club Band*, further pushing the limits that rock and pop music could reach. This back and forth was integral to creating the sound of the era that influenced the cultural movements at the time.

Though they were loved by the fans in their native England, their music also reached far outside of their island nation. In America they were loved so passionately that the group couldn't even hear what they were playing during concerts. Their giant show at Shea Stadium set a precedent for giant shows in stadiums around the globe. This precedent is followed even today, though with a better audio set-up, as the biggest names in music often bring their tours through giant stadiums. While in England they were the hometown boys who made it big, around the world they were *different*. The way they sounded and acted set them apart from the big musical artists that had made airways in America up to that point. Fans were swept up by the energy they brought to their performances.

> "I was in grade school; not a teenager -- so it wasn't about them being hot, it was about the fun; the overriding sense that they were having fun. And the freedom they expressed was palpable" (Leonard, 2014, p. 27).

Their reach didn't just end in America though. They inspired rock music and hippie culture movements throughout the world. In Russia many young people looked to music from the west as the iron curtain was slowly coming down. The Beatles were big enough that they inspired countless young Russian people to enter the world of rock music, including artists such as Andrei Makarevich who would create Russia's first big rock band, Time Machine. Makarevich's drive to become a musician was driven by the Beatles records his father had picked up while on business out of the country. In Leslie Woodhead's book *How the Beatles Rocked the Kremlin* Makarevich is quoted as saying:

> "It looked easy to play like they did, but of course it wasn't at all. We thought we could just get a guitar, grow our hair, get a Beatle jacket and we were them. And if you walked down Gorky Street with a guitar case you were a hero. So everybody forgot mathematics and sport and literature, and became Beatles" (2013).

Of course, their impact on cultural movements of the 60's and 70's was massive as well. the Beatles involvement in the Hippie movement introduced people to another way of thinking about drugs, sex, and global politics. Each of the Beatles had their own unique perspective in shaping the community. George Harrison's heavy interest in India and Hinduism not only brought Indian instruments to the forefront of rock and roll, but helped spread Hinduism to many westerners who may not have learned about the religion if Harrison had not done so first. Lennon pushed the button of global politics with his opinions and his willingness to debate for them. His relationship with Yoko Ono and their public protests helped set the stage for the hippie movement's focus on questioning governments decisions such as their willingness to go to war. McCartney and Starr would do their own work to push forward the idea of love and peace to their fans across the world, further helping usher in the hippie culture that would consume a large part of the 1970s.

The Beatles' messages and music changed people's perceptions of the world around them, but that wasn't the end of their cultural significance. Of course their image created a huge impact on the world as everyone wanted to look like a Beatle. From their bowl cut, clean suit boyband heartthrob days to their evolution into the style that would persist into the 70's; long hair, beards, and moustaches paired with colorful outfits. The fact that their influence had people changing their styles and outfits significantly twice just in the span of eight years is an incredible feat. This accomplishment alone shows how the Beatles permeated through the cultural zeitgeist at the time. They helped influence the world in so many facets that their impact as a social phenomena is unquestionable.

The Beatles Legacy

The influence of the Beatles on popular music remains a constant even to this day. Beatles contemporaries marveled at the group's tight harmonies, interesting chord selection, and as time went on, the structure of their songs. Their artistic vision influenced rock music to this day. The Beatles are considered one of the first bands to create a concept album in rock with *Sgt. Peppers Lonely Hearts Club Band* (Burns, 2009). Paul's idea of creating a new image for themselves to escape the imposing expectation placed on the Beatles helped other future bands focus on a theme for their albums and incorporate changes in their image to coincide. Bands such as Pink Floyd in the 1970's and My Chemical Romance in the 2000's would create their own spin on the idea of the concept album thanks to rock groups such as the Beatles' first attempts. *Sgt. Pepper* has also made tons of musical innovations for the rock genre that we would see for years to come. Techniques such as their focus on multi-track recording and having songs roll into each other rather than have silence cut in between influenced how future rock bands would record their own albums.

The Beatles also continue to live on top of the sales charts. The group holds the top spot for albums sold worldwide to this day with over 650 million units sold. No other individual or group has come close to that number, and with record sales becoming the secondary form of consuming music next to streaming, it seems that the Beatles will hold that record for many years to come. It doesn't seem like they are losing any popularity either. In 2009, the Beatles received over 1.7 billion streams through just nine months of the year on Spotify (Beech, 2019). That number comes from just *one* streaming service. With their music streaming on all of the major streaming services around the world, it is likely that the total global number is even higher amongst all platforms. Another peculiar statistic from the 1.7 billion Beatles songs streamed on Spotify, is that 30% of those plays were from people in the 18-24 demographic and 17% from the 25-29 demographic (Beech, 2019). On one hand, this might not be too surprising because of course young people are the ones most frequently using streaming applications. However, the fact that 47% of the 1.7 billion listens on Spotify came from people under thirty bodes well for the cultural significance and legacy of the Fab Four.

Ultimately, the Beatles influence lives on through their music and their image. One way of maintaining that their legacy can continue into the future is through the use of parody and covers. The Beatles have been a constant subject for parody for as long as the group has been a cultural icon. Jokes playing on their image, music, and messaging have been constant for years, and show no signs of slowing down. Popular television shows such as The Simpsons have parodied the Fab Four and play up their referential actions for the sake of humor. One of the first big parodies of the Beatles were the comedy group focused on imitating them known as The Rutles. The fictional 'Prefab Four' were conceived by Monty Python member Eric Idle and collaborator Neil Innes in the mid 70's for a British television sketch show where the group would sing songs that were familiar, but perhaps stranger than their famous counterparts (Spitz, 2013). Instead of "Penny Lane" there was "Doubleback Alley." Rather than crying for "Help", The Rutles were exclaiming "Ouch." While The Rutles were found both as live-action and an animated group, their popularity grew no matter the medium they found themselves in. So popular in fact that they released films, albums and even went on tour.

Their music also lives on today through artists who continue to cover songs written by the Beatles. It is difficult to go through a week without hearing a song by the Beatles or a cover of one of their songs either on the radio, on a streaming service, or even in commercials. There have been so many covers of their song catalogue, you can easily find lists ranking the best versions of Beatles songs covered by other artists reaching into the hundreds. It is interesting that artists today are trying to achieve the popularity necessary to succeed in the entertainment business because that is exactly how the Beatles started their journey. In fact some of the Beatles biggest hits have been songs they have covered themselves. Cover songs have had a long history of propelling pop groups into the charts, and the covers of the Beatles songs is evidence that the group has assisted in upholding the cover songs legacy in popular music. The Beatles original songs remain relevant to this day due to the wonderful songwriting that can be found throughout their entire track catalogue.

The Beatles are also remembered in a form of reimagination that are the Beatles tribute bands. Tribute artists are people who do everything in their ability to imitate a musician or musical group and tour around the globe for undying fandoms. As far as Beatles tribute groups, it is a particularly difficult task.

Not only do the members of the Beatles tribute band have to be more than competent musicians, but they must replicate the Fab Four's image, and their quirky on stage humour in order to allow the crowd to suspend their disbelief for a moment and accept the tribute group as the Beatles. The many tribute groups that don the look of the fab four and tour across the world to appease Beatles fans everywhere.

Conclusion

There is no question that the Beatles are one of the most influential bands in history. From their tight suit and moptop hair days to their psychedelic rock to their final rooftop concert, this band is nearly universally recognized for their influence and legacy throughout the ages. The four boys from Liverpool left their marks on history, both together and separately. Though their partnership as the Beatles only lasted eight years, those eight years were chock full of adventure, music, politics, relationships, drugs, movies, and more. Hundreds of thousands of books can be (and likely have) been filled with the exploits of the Beatles, and no doubt hundreds more will be written in the future. Though we have only covered a brief history of the Beatles and their impact on the world, as we delve into the next section of this book, we will be exploring specific moments in immense detail to help us better understand the songs they influenced, and the influences the songs then had on the world. If you took only one thing from this section of the book, let it be this: the Beatles' global impact was sensational during the 1960s, and continues to be so today in a wide variety of exciting, interesting, and unexpected ways.

Section 2: The Songs and Stories of the Beatles

Introduction

To say that there is a surefire way of establishing a list of the best Beatles songs that tell stories or that have fascinating stories attached to them is to tell a complete and utter mistruth. With the long list of Beatles songs, and the even longer list of stories to attach to them, there could be any number of lists of Beatles songs of this nature, and they would all be completely valid and correct. That said, each person, or group of people, will have specific reasons for choosing the songs and lists that they do, and before we jump into the songs of our choosing, it only makes sense for us to explain the logic behind the songs we selected and the order we selected them in.

There are two focuses that we took when considering which songs we would include in our list of storytelling Beatles songs. The first focus was on the songs that told stories, like "Maxwell's Silver Hammer" and "She's Leaving Home." These songs would allow us to explore the actual storytelling techniques utilized by (primarily) Lennon and McCartney, while also taking the time to explore the historical events that brought the songs to life. Our second focus was on the ways in which stories about the Beatles or events that the Beatles experienced resulted in Beatles songs, like "I am the Walrus" and "Misery." Exploring these songs and stories provides us with some of the context for events that the Beatles were experiencing around the times they were writing these songs. Through this historical context, we can better understand the factors that went into their songwriting.

Because it's so incredibly difficult to limit ourselves to a short list of songs, it was imperative that we include a short 'honourable mentions' list: one that would allow us to explore songs that fit closely, but not closely enough inside of the parameters that we had chosen. Songs like "Helter Skelter," whose story emerged by no fault of the Beatles themselves, and "Glass Onion," which was written for Beatles conspiracy theorists since John Lennon had such derision for them, still have fascinating context and stories that deserve to be heard and enjoyed by Beatles fans. The songs included in our honourable mentions section were agonized over by the authors because, of course, it's incredibly difficult to pick just a few songs to include when so many incredible, inspirational, and fun songs exist to choose from.

With all this in mind, we are terribly excited to humbly present our selection of Beatles songs that either tell stories in engaging ways or Beatles songs that have particularly intriguing stories surrounding their writing. The following 15 songs are, in our opinion, the stories that best reflect the storytelling of the Beatles, and we are delighted to share their stories with you. In that case, dear reader, without any further ado, it's time to jump into Beatles songs and Beatles history with the first song in our list: "Misery."

Misery

The world is treating me bad

Misery

I'm the kind of guy

Who never used to cry

The world is treatin' me bad

Misery

I've lost her now for sure

I won't see here no more

It's gonna be a drag

Misery

I'll remember all the little things we've done

Can't she see she'll always be the only one, only one?

Send her back to me

'Cause everyone can see

Without her I will be

In misery

I'll remember all the little things we've done

She'll remember and she'll miss her only one, lonely one

Send her back to me

'Cause everyone can see

Without her I will be

In misery

Oh, ooo, ooo in misery

Ooo, my misery

La, la, la, la, la, la

Misery

Misery isn't one of the more well-known Beatles songs, nor is it a particularly complicated song; on the surface, it appears to be a song about a boy who is down on his luck and sad because he lost a girl. 'Misery' is an early Beatles tune, released on their first album, *Please Please Me*. For many listeners, this tune is a preppy outlook on a lost love, with the words and the music in a disconnect: sad lyrics with upbeat music. This tune, however, has a much deeper background which, though is first expressed in this song, will continue to grow throughout future Beatles and post-Beatles songs, particularly for John and Paul. In our exploration of this song, we'll take a dive into the point in Beatles history during which this song was written, the fascinating dichotomy between lyrics and music, the history behind the words, and a quick discussion into how those themes would continue to manifest in later Beatles music.

First, some context. "Misery" was written in 1963, at a point where the Beatles had reached the British Top 20 with "Love Me Do," but hadn't yet completed a full LP. Up to this point, the band had reached success not only with Lennon-McCartney songs, but also with covers of songs like "My Bonnie" and "When the Saints go Marching In" - of course, to fit with the early Beatles image, these songs were given a rock'n'roll treatment instead of their typical, traditional feel. In the early 1960s, the Beatles had lost Stu Stucliffe on bass, and replaced Pete Best with Ringo Starr. In addition, they'd gained a manager, Brian Epstein, who was working with - and sometimes fighting against - the unruly group to get them an image and a reputation that didn't include things like yelling at the audience and, a pastime favoured by John Lennon, belching into the microphone (Burrows, 2012). the Beatles were working their way up the ladder, but they really hadn't gotten far yet.

It was in these early stages that the Beatles - pre-Ringo Starr - met with their first rejection - "one of pop music's most celebrated errors in judgement" (Burrows, 2012). the Beatles had recorded 15 tracks for Decca, one of the biggest record companies in Britain, but the head of Decca declined to sign the four boys from Liverpool to a contract. A bigger misjudgement, there has never been. Later, of course, the boys signed with George Martin for a five-year contract, starting with the single "Love Me Do" which was their first song to reach the British Top 20.

1963 began with the height of "Please Please Me" becoming a hit single, and the Beatles taking on their first television appearance, shocking and exciting the world with their image:

> The band, with their "mop-top" fringes and buttoned up suits, presented an image that clearly set them apart from other groups. Above all, the Beatles refused to appear mean and moody like so many other rock'n'rollers: instead, they bounced around the television screen with beaming grins. This didn't look like a choreographed act, it looked as if they were four lads having a good time. And it was very infectious (Burrows, 2012, p. 49).

February of 1963 entered the Beatles into their first ever national tour - though they weren't the headlining act. Helen Shapiro led the tour, and was a huge influence in the creation of the song 'Misery,' but not for the reasons we might think. Shapiro had wanted to be a singer since she was young, and had gone to the Maurice Burman School of Modern Pop Singing as well as joined a few local bands as early as age ten. She was signed to Columbia Records, and hit number three on the UK charts with her first single 'Don't Treat Me Like a Child' (Dowse, 2011). At the young age of fourteen, Shapiro was one of Britain's top female artists.

It was also at this time, while the Beatles were opening for Helen Shapiro, that they established that they wanted to branch out and write new material - to prove that they were more than just a cover band. Though they did have some Lennon-McCartney originals on their album, it also had covers, and they wanted to prove that they could write as well as they could sing. Interestingly:

> In early 1963, this was a far from normal move for a British act. Terry Dene, Billy Fury, Tommy Steele, Marty Wilde and Adam Faith had all recorded songs written by professional "Tin Pan

Alley" [sic] writers and tried to affect an American look and sound. Often they covered singles that had just become hits in America (Turner, 2015, p. 26-27).

"Misery" was written while the Beatles were on the second leg of their tour with Helen Shapiro; in fact, the song was originally written for Shapiro to sing. Now, there are two contesting stories about what happened with the song, seeing as Shapiro never ended up singing it. According to Shapiro, she had no say in whether or not she got to record the song: the decision was made long before news of the song reached her. She said that:

> John and Paul certainly offered 'Misery' to me first, through Norrie [Shapiro's A&R manager], but I didn't know anything about it until I met them on the first day of the tour (February 2, Bradford, Yorks). Apparently he'd turned it down even though I hadn't heard it (Shapiro, quoted in Turner, 2015, p. 28).

The song, then, was recorded by the Beatles on their *Please Please Me* album, but interestingly enough, still became the first Lennon-McCartney song to be covered by another artist. Kenny Lynch was one of the few black singers in British pop music at the time, and had several chart-topping singles in the early 1960s. He was also on tour with the Beatles and Shapiro, and remembers the discussion around "Misery" differently than Shapiro:

> One day, John and Paul called Helen up to the back of the coach and they played her 'Misery,' he says. She listened to it and said, 'I don't like it. It's too much of a man's song.' So I said 'I like it. I've got a free session when I go back [to record] on Tuesday. I'll do it for you'" (Lynch, quoted in Turner, 2015, p. 28).

Regardless of the circumstances, Lynch liked "Misery" and cemented himself in history as the first artist to cover a Lennon-McCartney original. Lynch did make a subtle yet important lyric change during his recording of the song, something we will discuss shortly as we get into the song itself.

Before we do so, we should briefly consider what Lennon and McCartney were attempting to do with the song, regardless of who recorded it - though in the end, they did record it in 11 takes on February 11, 1963.

Lennon and McCartney have both spoken about "Misery" and how it came about. McCartney suggested it was the duo's "first stab at a ballad" (McCartney, quoted in Turner, 2015, p. 28), once more pushing home the idea that the Beatles wanted to prove that they were more than just a cover band - they wanted to demonstrate their versatility as artists, musicians, and songwriters. It didn't matter that Shapiro's manager had requested that they write a song for her - for one reason or another, she wasn't going to record it, so the Beatles made the best of it by recording the song themselves.

Music critic Ian McDonald believed that "Misery" represented "a droll portrait of adolescent self-pity" (2005, p. 70-71). His analysis truly was perfect, because it summed up the song well. "Misery" is self-pitying when one considers the lyrics, but to consider the music, beat, and general energy provides us with a very different outlook on the song. "Misery" began a well-used tradition of sad lyrics layered on upbeat music that was used by the Lennon and McCartney writing team on a few occasions, as well as by McCartney again later in his career. It also tagged onto the popular function of preludes, and offered a layer of opportunity to look into Lennon's past: something that would arise in many, many Beatles tunes in the future. For now, let's begin by considering the song itself.

"Misery" is played at a tempo of 133 beats per minute, and as we discussed at the beginning of this book, tempo plays a large part in providing energy to a song. Slower songs have less energy and often feel more melancholy, whereas faster songs provide higher, more feel-good energy. In fact, Dutch neuroscientist Jacob Jolij was commissioned to do research on what makes the ultimate 'feel good' song, and his research will help us understand the reason that though "Misery" has sad lyrics, it has a good, upbeat feel to it anyway.

Jolij's research established the FGI, or Feel Good Index, for various songs, which allowed him to determine which aspects of a song impact its feel-good energy (Kim, 2015). He established that the positive references in the song's lyrics, its tempo in beats per minute, and its key all had large impacts on how energetic a song would end up being. "Misery," then, would have a high score in the tempo category, since its tempo is 133 beats per minute, and the "average pop song has a tempo of 116 beats per minute" (Kim, 2015). Does this make it a feel-good song, though? Let's consider the next category: key.

Though we discussed key signatures in the introduction to this book, we will give a quick recap to ensure that there is a complete understanding of the impact of key signatures on a song. We have to remember that "the association of musical keys with specific emotional or qualitative characteristic was fairly common prior to the 20th century. It was part of the shared cultural experience of those who made, performed and listened to music" (University of Michigan, n.d.). In that way, we all have a sense of musical key and emotion ingrained in our heads, likely without even knowing it. This is just one of the ways that we can feel the emotion of a song, without necessarily being able to verbalize why a song makes us feel a certain way.

'Misery' is played in the key C major. Now, this key plays a big part in the dissociation between the lyrics of the song and the song itself, because the key C major is "completely pure. Its character is: innocence, simplicity, naïvety, children's talk" (University of Michigan, n.d.). The character of C major ties into Ian McDonald's review of the song, in that it feels naive and childish, but also innocent and simple. In general, songs that are written in major keys feel happier than songs written in minor keys, but C major specifically brings out earnestness and innocence. Though the lyrics of "Misery" denote sadness, the key signature of the song works against the lyrics, creating a dissonance between happy and sad.

And so, on the Feel Good Index, we have key and tempo working in the favour of feel good, but then we have the lyrics. Now, the lyrics in this song are worth exploring for a few reasons: mostly because even though they are sung with a sense of boyish optimism, they reveal something about John Lennon and his childhood that would come out in much of his songwriting for the remainder of his life. The boyish optimism, of course, was characteristic of the Beatles at this point in time, as they were building rapport as an energetic, smiling, and, well, boyish band. Let's take a closer look at some of the lyrics and see what they can tell us.

The very first line of the song relates to what was, at the time, a new tradition in songwriting - using a preface. The line "the world is treating me bad, misery" acted as a prelude, much like other songs at that time, like Bobby Vee's 'Take Good Care of my Baby,' and Dion's 'Runaround Sue.' This line demonstrates both a recognition on Lennon and McCartney's side of a popular method of starting a song, and a desire for their songs to be seen in a similar light as the aforementioned songs. Not only that; the line also sums up the entirety of the 'mood' of the song, or the mood of the lyrics at least. In essence, it tells the story of the song in seven words.

The first line also happens to be the line that Kenny altered when he recorded the song. Instead of using the 'world,' Kenny sang that 'you've been treating me bad,' which changes the song in both a subtle and not-so-subtle way. Let's consider the impact of 'the world is treating me bad.' This is a theme that would return over and over again in Lennon's writing in particular, as it sounds more all-encompassing and ominous to the listener. In addition, as Steve Turner (2015) notes, the line verges on paranoia: the entire world, and everything in it, is doing the mistreating. But how does this relate to John Lennon?

John Lennon's childhood played a particularly poignant part in all of his work, but particularly in later Beatles songs and into his solo career. "Misery" hints at this part of his life that he hid behind his early-Beatles grin - but what was it that Lennon was hiding? Let's explore some of Lennon's early history, as well as some of his post-Beatles interviews and songs that spoke to the feelings about his childhood that he'd been holding inside for so long.

John Winston Lennon was born on October 9, 1940 in Liverpool to Julia and Alfred (Freddy) Lennon. Alfred was away at sea during the time of his son's birth, setting a precedent of absenteeism during his son's life, something that impacted John deeply throughout his life. Alfred spent very few trips visiting Liverpool to see his wife and child, instead spending time "interned at Ellis Island and [...] serving a sentence for desertion at a British military prison in North Africa" (Burrows, 2012, p. 10). He never wanted to be a part of the war, and eventually established he never wanted to be a family man either: "Freddy did reappear briefly in 1945 and tried to persuade John and Julia to move to New Zealand with him. When Julia refused, John was given the option of choosing between his two parents" (Burrows, 2012, p. 10). John stayed with his mother, and watched his father walk out of his life.

Julia, on the other hand, was physically present for John's childhood, but was "temperamental, ill-prepared for raising a son on her own, and frankly not that interested in it" (Sullivan & Andreas, 2013, p. 10). She stayed fairly distant from her son during his childhood, and spent most of his childhood sending him to spend time with his aunts while she worked at a cafe on Penny Lane. As Lennon grew older, he ended up seeing his mother more as an older sister; he was living with his aunt Mimi, who we will discuss momentarily, and his mother was the influence that "told him the kind of things that he wanted to hear, such as not to worry about homework or what might happen in the future" (Burrows, 2012, p. 11). Lennon always had a difficult relationship with his mother: in a way, she had abandoned him as a parent, but had become something like a close friend; in fact, she was the one who encouraged his love for music and taught him to play the banjo. It was on July 15, 1958, that tragedy struck, and Julia was killed. She was walking home, but was hit by "a drunk learner-driver, an off-duty policeman named Eric Clague. Drinking and driving was not illegal at the time, and Clague's testimony stated that she simply walked out of the hedge-lined central reservation straight in front of him. He was acquitted of all charges" (Burrows, 2012, p. 11). At the time, Lennon was 17; he had "understandably, developed complex feelings towards her that would haunt him [after her death]" (Sullivan & Andreas, 2013, p. 10).

For most of his childhood, Lennon lived with his Aunt Mimi, his mother's sister, who he absolutely worshipped. Mimi was "something of a disciplinarian" (Burrows, 2012, p. 11) and was a sharp contrast to the flighty encouragement that Julia provided to John. Mimi encouraged John to read and write, and tried to break him of his rebellious tendencies; by the time he reached his teenage years, "Mimi [...] began to dread the phone calls from the school secretary detailing her charge's latest petty misdemeanors" (Burrows, 2012, p. 11). Mimi did provide some encouragement for John and his music, since she was the one to buy him his first guitar. His guitar came with a warning from her, that "the guitar's very well, John, but you'll never make a living out of it" (Sullivan & Andreas, 2013, p. 10). Oh how wrong Aunt Mimi was.

These main figures in John's early life had a large impact on the rest of his life, demonstrated within his songs. For example, the Beatles tune "Julia" was written about John's mother, because Lennon wanted to "write a song about the childhood I never really had with my mother" (Lennon, quoted in Marchese, 2016). Donovan, the artist that helped Lennon write "Julia" remembers the writing of the song:

> [Lennon] asked me to help him with the images that he could use in lyrics for a song about this subject. So I said, "Well, when you think of the song, where do you imagine yourself?" And John said, "I'm at a beach and I'm holding hands with my mother and we're walking together." And I helped him with a couple of lines, "Seashell eyes / windy smile" — for the Lewis Carroll, Alice in Wonderland feel that John loved so much. And the song, which you may know, is the amazing "Julia" [Donovan, quoted in Marchese, 2016).

Julia had a massive impact on her son's life, and her death was one of the reasons that he leaned towards feeling like 'the world is treating me bad.' Lennon didn't even get one of his parents to stick around in a parental role; instead, they were both absent in one way or another. "Julia" wasn't the only song that Lennon went on to write about his mother: he also wrote the aptly-named "Mother" and the gut-wrenching tune "My Mummy's Dead." This demonstrates Lennon's connection to his mother and how strongly he felt about her death: ""I lost her twice," Lennon said. "Once as a five-year-old when I was moved in with my auntie. And once again when she actually physically died"" (Rolling Stone, 2020).

It's important to have this background information about Lennon's history as we consider the tune "Misery" because it allows us to delve deeper into our understanding of the song itself, and the impact of the line 'the world is treating me bad,' particularly when considering the fact that Kenny changed those lyrics in his cover of the song which gave the cover a different feeling than the original Lennon-McCartney tune.

Now, the lyrics of "Misery" themselves were clearly written more in regards to a boyish crush or an early girlfriend, with the knowledge of Lennon's history and struggle with his emotions surrounding his mother, it isn't difficult to peel away the layer of romance from the song and see connections between John and Julia. For example 'I've lost her now for sure/I won't see her no more' could be a relation to the fact that Julia died and is certainly lost to John; similarly 'without her I will be in misery' could relate to John's sadness at the loss of his mother, particularly considering that because her killer was never charged, he never got a sense of closure after her death.

As we can see, though it may appear that the early Beatles songs focused on love and not much else, there are stories behind many of these songs that tell deeper and darker tales than just what is seen on the surface. Though "Misery" wasn't initially intended to be a Beatles song, and it may not have become one of the most popular Beatles songs, it has gone down in Beatles history as one of the first Beatles songs that delves into common themes that Lennon would return to over his career: paranoia, isolation, and loss. As we've discussed, there are many aspects that bring the song together in addition to its history, but this perky and happy song about losing someone close has been quite a curious and engaging song to explore.

Norwegian Wood

I once had a girl

Or should I say she once had me

She showed me her room

Isn't it good Norwegian wood?

She asked me to stay

And she told me to sit anywhere

So I looked around

And I noticed there wasn't a chair

I sat on a rug biding my time

Drinking her wine

We talked until two and then she said

"It's time for bed"

She told me she worked

In the morning and started to laugh

I told her I didn't

And crawled off to sleep in the bath

And when I awoke I was alone

This bird had flown

So I lit a fire

Isn't it good Norwegian wood?

At first glance "Norwegian Wood" may seem like a humble story about one friend visiting another's apartment. However, as the song tells its story, the song begins to take a darker turn. A part of the album *Rubber Soul*, the track helps push forward the will to grow as musicians that the Beatles displayed on every song that takes a spot in the tracklist. While many of the songs from this album show the groups desire to improve their musicianship through their multi-track recording methods and their instrumentation, "Norwegian Wood" is one of their first that really places an emphasis on the lyrics. While the song does play with the instrumentation the group used, as we will discuss later, the focus of the track is the story it tells, and how the lyrics contain set-ups to plot elements later in the song and play with it's audiences perceptions of it's characters.

"Norwegian Wood" is a song that holds two different meanings. One is the fictional story the song tells, of a man visiting a woman's home hoping for some romance to bloom only for nothing of the sort to appear. The other is related to the events of Lennon's personal life and what he was trying to convey through this song. While this is the case for many songs, "Norwegian Wood" is an interesting case because of just how much is known about it, along with the personal life of Lennon. By analyzing both the fictional story and the personal circumstances of a song we can learn about not only the song, but those who wrote it.

The lyrics of "Norwegian Wood" can be described as ambiguous. Nothing is explicitly stated, such as the man's objective is in visiting the woman's home or what exactly occurs at the end of the track. The lyrics also tend to focus on the unfamiliar space that our protagonist occupies, as the odd features of the apartment are mentioned throughout the song. While the song may not explain the events or ideas of the song directly, Norwegian Wood most definitely does tell a story once the listener pays attention to it's lyrics. A story of love, discomfort in new environments and relationships, and ultimately revenge.

"I once had a girl

Or should I say she once had me

She showed me her room

Isn't it good Norwegian wood? [...]"

The opening lines of "Norwegian Wood" already set the stage for the uncomfortable nature the protagonist finds themselves in. In recalling the past they mention that they "had a girl" only to show doubt in the very next line saying "she once had me." In these lines we see the idea of a relationship being possessive, or at least that one party is more infatuated in their partner than the other is. The listener is introduced to the situation and the context of it. The protagonist realizes that he was much more infatuated with her than she was with them, a love that would never be requited unbeknownst to them. Now with the context of their relationship, the next two lines introduce the listener to the current situation of the protagonist receiving an apartment tour from the woman. While the protagonist is being shown around by the girl, he notes that the wood found in her room is norwegian wood. This is an important note to set up the final lines of the song.

In the next section of the song, the listener is introduced to the strange nature of this woman's apartment as the protagonist notes that "there wasn't a chair. This displays the disconnect between the two, even though the protagonist is interested in her she seems to be much different than what he is used to. As the night continues they sit and talk two in the morning when she announces that she has to work in the morning, with the protagonist only mentioning that they don't have to work and their conversation ends with that. We see the further disconnect between the two characters as our protagonist, unsure of their situation and surroundings, goes to sleep in the bathtub.

"[...] And when I awoke I was alone

This bird had flown

So I lit a fire

Isn't it good Norwegian wood?"

The ending lines of the song allow the listener to interpret its meaning. Our protagonist wakes up in an empty apartment, the woman has left for work. The last two lines are ambiguous and mysterious. The protagonist lights a fire, but we are left to ask what they have lit on fire? They could have started one in a fireplace if the apartment was equipped with such. However, the line "Isn't it good, Norwegian Wood" implies something more sinister. In this new context, the norwegian wood that makes up the woman's bedroom seems to be the wood that the protagonist has used to light the fire. This revelation brings up another question, one asking why the protagonist has lit the woman's apartment on fire? Had he gone mad? Was he angered by her not reciprocating his feelings? That is up to the listener to determine for themselves.

However, the mystery of this ending can be washed away by listening to accounts from McCartney and Lennon regarding the song. In fact this song began it's creation while Lennon was enjoying a skiing vacation St. Moritz, Switzerland (MacDonald, 2007, p. 163), where he was trying to put his feelings to paper regarding his personal life. More precisely, Lennon was attempting to express his adulterous relationships to his then wife, Julia. It has been thought that "Norwegian Wood" took form based on one of his many affairs (Turner, 2005, 89). Lennon's reason for writing the song went unrealized to his peers, who took the many elements from the song just as fiction or focused on the parts of the song that seemed to be based on other elements of Lennon's life. For example, former Quarrymen member Pete Shotton felt that the burning wood element of the song was pulled from John's habit of burning furniture in their younger years when they had no money for coal, and his referring guests to sleep in the bathtub (Turner, 2005, p. 89).

While "Norwegian Wood" is often attributed primarily to Lennon in the McCartney/Lennon writing duo. This has often been contested by the two however. Lennon in the past had said that the track was 100% his, while McCartney is adamant that he had a hand in penning the song's lyrics, specifically the ending lyrics (MacDonald, 2007, p. 164). It has also been suggested that Lennon approached McCartney after his trip and asked him for help in finishing the song, so Paul suggested that the story should be developed through a woman leading a man on, ending with the man setting her apartment ablaze (Turner, 2005, p. 89).

> [...] Norwegian Wood is the first Beatle song in which the lyric is more important than the music. In the spirit of the teasing narratives in Dyla's recent albums, with their enigmatic women and hints of menace, it was hailed as a breakthrough -- and, despite the fact that its admired elusiveness was mostly a product of bluff and evasion, found its way into a book of modern verse (MacDonald, 2007).

While "Norwegian Wood" is one of the Beatles first songs to be more focused on its lyrical content and storytelling, the music accompanying the lyrics also provides a huge first for not only the Beatles, but rock music in general. This is because of George Harrison's sitar that appears on the track. The use of the sitar, wailing in between Lennon's vocal performance and laying background sounds during, provided rock music it's first taste of the sitar. The introduction of different instruments from cultures outside of the western mainstream helped sweep in an era of experimentation in sounds amongst the rock and pop genres. Contemporaries of the group such as the Rolling Stones would follow suit and incorporate the sound of the sitar into one of their biggest songs, "Paint It Black."

Though not considered one of the Beatles mega hits, "Norwegian Wood" still gained an incredible amount of success at the time of its release. While it is easy to point out that any track with the name Beatles on it could have sold well at the time, it stands as a testament to the musicianship of the group to continue to grow and push the boundaries of their genre and songwriting. Today the song is remembered fondly by fans, with Mojo magazine ranking it the 19th best Beatles song. Outside of music, the song's title was borrowed for the title of Haruki Murakami's novel "Norwegian Wood" in which it is one of the main characters' favourite songs.

As it stands today "Norwegian Wood" may not be a Beatles song you hear on the radio in your day to day life, but is one revered by fans and critics alike to this day. Sure, it is easy to underestimate this seemingly humble song when it follows the rambunctious "Drive My Car." However, that does not hamper the track's significance as an important section of Beatles history or as a piece of lyrical storytelling in early rock music. It is and will remain a historical token of the Beatles shift in approach to songwriting and lyrical content.

Paperback Writer

Paperback writer (paperback writer)

Dear Sir or Madam, will you read my book?

It took me years to write, will you take a look?

It's based on a novel by a man named Lear

And I need a job

So I want to be a paperback writer

Paperback writer

It's a dirty story of a dirty man

And his clinging wife doesn't understand

His son is working for the Daily Mail

It's a steady job

But he wants to be a paperback writer

Paperback writer

Paperback writer (paperback writer)

It's a thousand pages, give or take a few

I'll be writing more in a week or two

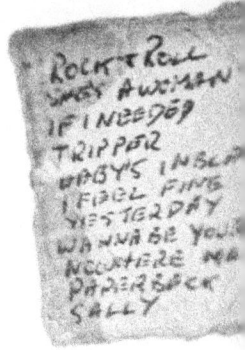

I could make it longer if you like the style

I can change it 'round

And I want to be a paperback writer

Paperback writer

If you really like it you can have the rights

It could make a million for you overnight

If you must return it you can send it here

But I need a break

And I want to be a paperback writer

Paperback writer

Paperback writer (paperback writer)

Paperback writer (paperback writer)

Paperback writer (paperback writer)

Paperback writer (paperback writer)

Paperback writer (paperback writer)

"Paperback Writer" is a curious Beatles song, because it delves away from Lennon & McCartney traditional storytelling territory: writing about love. In fact, according to Steve Turner, "Paperback Writer" was "the Beatles' first single not to have a love theme" (Turner, 2015, p. 151). Though *Revolver* was, unquestionably, the first album in which the Beatles truly began to truly open themselves up to new artistic opportunities, the fact that this song is so non-traditional in a variety of ways is truly worth exploring. Between the actual topic of the song, the way in which the song is written, and the way the historical story of publishing and the paperback book is intertwined within the story, there are many reasons to consider this song as a breakthrough in musical storytelling, particularly for Paul McCartney.

The way that this song came into existence is interesting in itself: it wasn't the brain child of a typical Lennon & McCartney songwriting session, nor was its idea brought on by a particular fascination with the world of publication. Instead, 'Paperback Writer' emerged from a conversation between Paul McCartney and his aunt Lil, wherein she questioned why all the songs he wrote and sang had to be about love. Auntie Lil's question to Paul was thus: "'why do you always write songs about love all the time? Can't you ever write about a horse or the summit conference or something interesting?'" (Auntie Lil, quoted in Whatley, 2020). Paul was inspired by this question, and went on to write something unlike anything the Beatles had ever performed before. There are a variety of stories as to how McCartney elected to write about paperbacks and writing from this conversation: Turner (2015) suggests that Paul simply seeing Ringo reading a book as being the inspiration, whereas Whatley (2020) cites Paul admitting that "the song was inspired when he read the story of a struggling author in The Daily Mail, a paper often found in Lennon's Weybridge home while the pair were writing."

Regardless of the reason for selecting this topic for his song, McCartney pushed on and began crafting a masterful tale about a writer wishing to sell his book to a publisher. Rumour has it that the song was based on a letter that was sent to Paul by an aspiring author, but to this author's knowledge, a rumor is as far as that story goes. Yet McCartney's choice to write this song in the form of a letter is another curious artistic choice, as it was atypical for that particular age. That being said, the Beatles weren't shying away from the unconventional, and when McCartney suggested the letter style to Lennon, he agreed that it was a good idea. Barry Miles quotes McCartney in his biography *Many Years from Now*:

> I arrived at Weybridge and told John I had this idea of trying to write off to a publishers to become a Paperback Writer, and I said, 'I think it should be written like a letter.' I took a bit of paper out and I said it should be something like, 'Dear Sir or Madam, as the case may be…' and I proceeded to write it just like a letter in front of him, occasionally rhyming it. And John, as I recall, just sat there and said, 'Oh, that's it,' 'Uhuh,' 'Yeah.' I remember him, his amused smile, saying, 'Yes, that's it, that'll do.' Quite a nice moment: 'Hmm, I've done right! I've done well!' And then we went upstairs and put the melody to it. John and I sat down and finished it all up, but it was tilted towards me, the original idea was mine. I had no music, but it's just a little bluesy song, not a lot of melody" (McCartney cited in Miles, 1997).

In the end, the letter style for this song was not only fitting, but also poetic: the style was a representation of the actual form in which an author would submit a query letter to a prospective literary agent or publisher. In order to receive representation from a literary agent or publisher, an author must submit a short 'query' letter introducing themselves and their work to their desired representative - McCartney's letter begins by pleading "dear sir or madam, will you read my book," effectively replicating the basis of a query letter within his song. This accurate reference has been noticed, and appreciated, by much of the literary community, including literary agent Jon Gibbs who wrote a satiric response to McCartney's letter. His highly entertaining response noted that:

> I detect a lyrical symmetry in the way you wrote your letter which makes me wonder if your efforts might find better reward in the

field of poetry, or even songwriting. Perhaps you could set your letter of enquiry to music, though I'm not sure a song about wanting to write paperback books is exactly the sort of thing young people would listen to. These days, everything on the hit parade seems to be a variation on the theme of love (2011).

It's fair to say that most songs aren't directed towards the literary community, so it makes sense that the literary community would fundamentally appreciate the reasonable attempt at accuracy that McCartney made within 'Paperback Writer' while still maintaining the important musical aspects of the song.

Not only was McCartney fairly accurate in his production of a query letter, he also shined a light on the history of paperback publishing, In order to really appreciate the beauty of 'Paperback Writer,' let's take a moment and dive into some fascinating aspects of paperback publishing - a side quest that will not only help us better understand why 'Paperback Writer' is such a treasure, but that will also help us understand the history of the type of book you are holding in your hands at this exact moment.

Paperback books date back as far as the 17th century, when newly invented machines like the steam press allowed for fairly inexpensive reproduction of short books - and we have to remember that before the printing press, all book replication was done by hand. In the United States especially, the publishing industry was slow to start - it seemed that no matter how many books publishers put out, they simply weren't selling. Now, that's not at all a reflection of literacy rates within the United States at that time. As Alexis Madrigal notes: " by 1940, UNESCO estimated that 95 percent of adults in America were literate. No, it's just that the vast majority of adults were not considered to be part of the cultural enterprise of book publishing. People read stuff (the paper, the Bible, comic books), just not what the publishers were putting out" (2012).

As Madrigal's fascinating article explains, there were only approximately 500 bookstores in all of the United States in the early 1930s. It's a curious phenomenon, because though folks continued to read things like the Bible, they weren't buying traditional hardcover books. Thankfully, the book publishing industry took a huge leap in the right direction; interestingly, this leap happened during the second world war, a time when the industry believed it simply wouldn't be able to survive. The big change came from Allen Lane, a London publisher. Allen Corlett tells the story quite wonderfully:

> The story goes that Allen Lane, Chairman of The Bodley Head, a London publisher, was returning by train from a weekend in the country with one of his authors — Agatha Christie — and her husband. The Bodley Head, like many publishers of the time, was suffering precipitously declining sales, and had been since the onset of the Depression, and Lane was looking for a way to save his troubled business. Browsing the station kiosks for something to read while he waited for the train, he could find nothing to buy except slick magazines and low-quality paperback fiction (like the cheaply produced Routledge's Railway Classic reprint series). It occurred to him that good quality fiction and nonfiction might find a wider readership if only books were more affordable, and on July 30th, 1935 he introduced the Penguin imprint to an unsuspecting world (2001).

When Lane began offering paperback books - the first of which was written by Agatha Christie - for the same price as a pack of cigarettes, the paperback book industry boomed: suddenly everyone was voraciously reading paperback books. The fact that they were paperback, and extremely inexpensive (about the equivalent of four cents nowadays), meant that they were seen as more single-use or disposable than the expensive hardcover books that still sold less. Soldiers heading off to war couldn't warrant taking a hardcover book with them, but they could take a small paperback book that fit into their pocket when they needed to get back to work. Paperbacks were more convenient and affordable for the everyday population, hence their incredible popularity across the world.

To bring the story back to the question at hand, it makes sense then that McCartney sings 'I want to be a paperback writer," because the distinction between hardcover and paperback is the distinction between reaching a niche market or the mass market with a story. Anyone who wanted to reach a large market with their story would have to be writing paperback books: the hardcover books simply didn't have the same amount of reach. This simple fact may not have been recognized by many of the people who listened to 'Paperback Writer,' which in itself demonstrates the many levels upon which the stories that this song tells can be understood.

On a basic level, 'Paperback Writer' is a song about a man who wants to sell his manuscript to a publisher. Once we delve deeper, we realize that 'Paperback Writer' shares a fascinating narrative about the book publishing industry, and how paperback books ended up being mass-produced due to their convenience, cheap printing price, cheap purchasing price, and highly enjoyable stories. Even references within the song, like "the man named Lear" referencing Edward Lear - a poet who John Lennon had been compared to after writing his book "In His Own Write" - and "the Daily Mail," a popular newspaper that Lennon often read, insinuate that there is a deeper understanding to be had of this seemingly open and shut story of a man wanting nothing more than to sell his book and become a paperback writer.

There are two distinct stories within this song as well: the story of the man who wants to be a published author, and the story of the publishing industry. The fact that McCartney can tell both stories in a memorable, catchy, and enjoyable song that lasts less than two-and-a-half minutes, is nothing short of incredible - as is the fact that his reference to the deeper story of the publishing industry is often missed by casual listeners. Considering that the predominant Beatles song theme until this point had been love, this jump into realism and historical storytelling was an exciting and new opportunity for the band to tell a new story, and a story that is not often told in song. Though there are millions of aspiring authors in this world, there are few stories about attempts to sell books to publishers or agents, and McCartney's song reflects deeply in the hearts of all authors who would like nothing more than to see their own handiwork on the shelves of a bookstore - whether it be in hardcover or paperback.

Lucy in the Sky with Diamonds

Picture yourself in a boat on a river

With tangerine trees and marmalade skies

Somebody calls you, you answer quite slowly

A girl with kaleidoscope eyes

Cellophane flowers of yellow and green

Towering over your head

Look for the girl with the sun in her eyes

And she's gone

Lucy in the sky with diamonds

Lucy in the sky with diamonds

Lucy in the sky with diamonds

Ah

Follow her down to a bridge by a fountain

Where rocking horse people eat marshmallow pies

Everyone smiles as you drift past the flowers

That grow so incredibly high

Newspaper taxis appear on the shore

Waiting to take you away

Climb in the back with your head in the clouds

And you're gone

Lucy in the sky with diamonds

Lucy in the sky with diamonds

Lucy in the sky with diamonds

Ah

Picture yourself on a train in a station

With plasticine porters with looking glass ties

Suddenly someone is there at the turnstile

The girl with the kaleidoscope eyes

Lucy in the sky with diamonds

Lucy in the sky with diamonds

Lucy in the sky with diamonds

Ah

Lucy in the sky with diamonds

Lucy in the sky with diamonds

Lucy in the sky with diamonds

Ah

Lucy in the sky with diamonds

Lucy in the sky with diamonds

Lucy in the sky with diamonds

"Lucy in the Sky with Diamonds" carries with it a fascinating and reasonably unknown story, in direct comparison to the story that people think is behind the song. The tune is quintessentially Lennon-esque, with a variety of psychedelic images provided throughout the song. Most people believe the song to be about drugs - the fact that the song's initials are LSD seems to push that theory along well - but the real story behind the song is particularly meaningful now that we see what happened to the real Lucy throughout her life. Within this section, we'll explore and refute the popular drug theory, learn about the true background of the song and about the real Lucy who inspired it, and explore some of the specific lyrics and how they are reminiscent of works by Lewis Carroll, a favourite author of Lennon. So, without further ado, let's explore the incredible work that is "Lucy in the Sky with Diamonds."

To begin, let's take a moment to explore Lennon's connection to the psychedelic and how his literature preferences inspired specific aspects of this song. This is something that we will explore again, with a bit of a different lens, when we discuss "I am the Walrus," but it is important for us to take a moment here and recognize that these concepts and words in the song didn't come from a drug-induced haze; instead, they were brought about through Lennon's preferred literature and television. To do so, let's take some time to learn about one of Lennon's favourite authors, and some of his most famous works. The author? Lewis Carroll.

Charles Lutwidge Dodgson, or Lewis Carroll as the world knew him, was born in 1832 in England and died in 1896 in Surrey. He was one of eleven children, and since he was the oldest boy and the third-oldest child in the family, as he grew up, he found himself entertaining his younger siblings by creating games and stories to keep them entertained and engaged. He began writing at age 12, though the majority of his early works were not published until after his death. He was particularly bright, and found his love for mathematics and classical studies throughout his studies - this interest led him to become a tutor at Christ Church in Oxford.

It was through this tutoring position that he met the girl that would inspire him to write his greatest literary achievement: *Alice in Wonderland*. Alice Liddell was the daughter of the dean of Christ Church, and since Dodgson had such affinity to children from growing up with so many siblings, he was often asked to entertain Alice Liddell and her two sisters - with proper chaperoning, of course. It would be prudent at this point in our exploration to note that there is much discussion and debate about Dodgson and his interest in children; stemming from discussion about whether or not he was a bit too interested in Alice, who was quite young. Dodgson, interestingly enough, never married and remained a bachelor his whole life. Though this discussion isn't entirely prevalent to our discussion about "Lucy in the Sky with Diamonds," the authors felt it important to include this note about Dodgson to provide context for the discussions surrounding *Alice in Wonderland.*

As quoted by Roger Lancelyn Green, who has written and edited many books on Lewis Carroll, Alice Liddell distinctly remembered visiting Dodgson:

> [they] used to sit on the big sofa on each side of him, while he told us stories, illustrating them by pencil or ink drawings as he went along.…He seemed to have an endless store of these fantastical tales, which he made up as he told them, drawing busily on a large sheet of paper all the time. They were not always entirely new. Sometimes they were new versions of old stories; sometimes they started on the old basis, but grew into new tales owing to the frequent interruptions which opened up fresh and undreamed-of possibilities (Liddell, cited in Green, 2021).

Inspired to tell stories of Alice, Dodgson would make up fantastic stories to tell the girl whenever he saw her. When she asked him to write out the adventures for her, he was only too happy to oblige, and write a story based on a picnic that he and Alice had shared. Once he provided the written copy to Alice Liddell, he essentially forgot entirely about the topic. As Roger Green explains, the book would have been forgotten if a novelist visiting the Liddell home had not found it:

But the novelist Henry Kingsley, while visiting the deanery, chanced to pick it up from the drawing-room table, read it, and urged Mrs. Liddell to persuade the author to publish it. Dodgson, honestly surprised, consulted his friend George Macdonald, author of some of the best children's stories of the period. Macdonald took it home to be read to his children, and his son Greville, aged six, declared that he "wished there were 60,000 volumes of it" (Green, 2021).

From there, the book was edited, published, and published again, growing to the worldwide phenomenon that is *Alice in Wonderland*. John Lennon remembers the impact that *Alice in Wonderland* and its companion *Through the Looking Glass* had on him as a child, and purported to read them at least once a year (Turner, 2015, p. 181). According to Lennon, these books impacted the way he thought about himself and the thoughts he had: "he claimed that it was partly through reading them that he realized the images in his own mind weren't indications of insanity. 'Surrealism to me is reality' he said. 'Psychedelic vision is reality to me and always was'" (Lennon, quoted in Turner, 2015, p. 181).

Of course, *Alice in Wonderland* wasn't Lewis Carroll's only psychedelic literary work; in fact, his poem "The Hunting of the Snark" has been deemed "nonsense literature in the highest order" (Green, 2021). Since Lennon enjoyed Carroll's writing style, and had a preference for surrealism and surreal humour, it makes sense that Lennon would have read more than just the *Alice in Wonderland* books that Carroll wrote, though Lennon has confirmed that the most influential work of Carroll's for him was *Alice in Wonderland*. Of course, Lennon's preference for surrealism wasn't solely fulfilled through the works of Lewis Carroll; he also enjoyed a British radio comedy show called *The Goon Show*, which "lampooned establishment figures, attacked post-war stuffiness, and popularized surreal humour" (Turner, 2015, p. 181).

Now that we have a basic understanding of where Lennon's preference for psychedelics and surrealism emerged, let's take a moment to explore the actual origins of the song, which will then help us refute the popular theory that the song is about an LSD trip. Once we've established the actual story, we can take some time to explore some of the lyrics themselves and what they represented - to Lennon and McCartney and to the rest of the world.

"Lucy in the Sky with Diamonds" emerged from a drawing that a young Julian Lennon showed his father. As Steve Turner explains: "one afternoon early in 1967, Julian Lennon came home from his nursery school with a coloured drawing that he said was of his classmate, four-year-old Lucy O'Donnell. Explaining his artwork to his father, Julian said it was of 'Lucy - in the sky with diamonds'" (Turner, 2015, p. 181). John Lennon, of course, was inspired by the psychedelic image, and proceeded to write a song, which he titled based on his son's description. Of course, as soon as the song was released and the public realized that the initials of the song spelled LSD, there was no question in their minds that the song wasn't about anything but drugs. To the end of his life, however, Lennon maintained that the song was nothing more than a nonsensical song based on a drawing by his son. In an interview, when questioned about the song's meaning, Lennon explained:

> This is the truth: My son came home with a drawing and showed me this strange-looking woman flying around,"[...] "I said, 'What is it?' and he said, 'It's Lucy in the sky with diamonds,' and I thought, 'That's beautiful.' I immediately wrote a song about it. After the album had come out and the album had been published, someone noticed that the letters spelt out LSD and I had no idea about it. … But nobody believes me (Lennon, quoted in Runtagh, 2017).

As Runtagh later notes in the article, "Lennon was very forthright about the role drug use played in his songwriting" and "it seems out of character that Lennon would lie about the true origins of "Lucy in the Sky with Diamonds"" (Runtagh, 2017). That said, knowing Lennon's aversion to explaining the stories behind the songs, as we will run into when we learn about "I am the Walrus" and "Glass Onion," it simply makes sense that Lennon was, in fact, telling us the truth, and there are no intentional references to drugs within "Lucy in the Sky with Diamonds." It would be prudent of us, however, to take some time to learn about the real Lucy and how her life turned out, because when we explore this path, the song takes on a deeper meaning than Lennon himself could have ever intended.

Lucy O'Donnell had no idea that she was the inspiration for a Beatles song until she was in her mid-teens. She did, however, remember Julian Lennon: "I can remember him very well. I can see his face clearly. We used to sit alongside each other in proper old-fashioned desks." [...] "He was the bravest boy in school whom I recall jumping into a freezing swimming pool" (O'Donnell, quoted in Runtagh, 2017). She has been told that she and Julian were "little menaces" (Turner, 2015, p. 181) during their time at the school together, but remembers it and him fondly.

After Julian's parents split, he moved to a different school, and he and Lucy lost touch. It was during this time that Lucy learned about the part she played in the famous Beatles tune, but she learned about this after the infamous LSD rumour made its rounds, so she never really connected herself with the song. She remembers: "as a teenager, I made the mistake of telling a couple of friends at school that I was the Lucy in the song and they said, 'No, it's not you, my parents said it's about drugs.' And I didn't know what LSD was at the time, so I just kept it quiet, to myself" (O'Donnell, quoted in Runtagh, 2017).

Lucy and Julian met once, decades later, at one of Julian's concerts, but outside of that, the two remained separate, with Lucy enjoying her connection to the Beatles in a very silent way. Steve Turner recounts her life best:

> When she was 32, Lucy married her childhood sweetheart Ross
> Vodden, but her life was then blighted by a series of serious health
> problems starting with psoriatic arthritis which saw her confined
> to a wheelchair, and then continuing with kidney, liver, and spleen
> problems. At the age of 39, she was diagnosed with lupus and

several other auto-immune diseases which eventually confined her to bed (Turner, 2015, p. 182).

Lucy and Julian reconnected near the end of Lucy's life when Julian found out that Lucy had been diagnosed with lupus. "After hearing about her disease, Julian, who lives in France, sent her flowers and vouchers for use at a gardening center near her home in Surrey in southeast England, and frequently sent her text messages in an effort to buttress her spirits" (The Associated Press, 2009). It was during this time that Lucy came out of the shadows in regards to her connection to the Beatles, and ended up using the connection as a fundraising tool for St. Thomas' Lupus Trust. When Lucy passed away in 2009, Julian "wrote and recorded a song called 'Lucy' in her memory and a year later became a patron of St. Thomas' Lupus Trust" (Turner, 2015, p. 182), a cause he continues to support to this day. Lucy's fate added additional meaning to the song after her death; as if she is truly a girl with kaleidoscope eyes looking down on the world from beyond.

Now that we've explored the true story behind "Lucy in the Sky with Diamonds," let's take a moment to explore some of the lyrics and the writing of the song itself. Though this song was predominantly written by John Lennon, Paul McCartney did have some important input in the song's lyrics, and provided some of the psychedelic lyrics, which we will explore momentarily. John Lennon maintains that "the hallucinatory images in the song were inspired by the 'Wool and Water' chapter in Lewis Carroll's *Through the Looking Glass*, where Alice is taken down a river in a rowing boat by the Queen, who has changed into a sheep" (Turner, 2015, p. 181). With this in mind, let's take a deeper look at some of the specific lyrics, and how they bring the song together in one of the greatest musical psychedelic masterpieces of all time.

The song begins with two very important words; words that have profound impact on the song and its listeners. "Picture yourself" invites listeners to connect to the lyrics on a deep level, as it requests that they use their imaginations to picture the images that Lennon sings about, and put themselves in a situation where those images have come to life. "Picture yourself" takes the psychedelic nature of the song one step further, as it invites listeners in to be a part of the song, instead of a passive observer. In this way, the song feels to be a collaborative effort between singer and listener as the singer provides images for the listener to bring to life in their mind. As with much psychedelic work, no two listeners will see the images that Lennon sings about in the same way, thus creating an infinite amount of ways that the song can be interpreted. Unique interpretations for each listener create deeper connections to the song, which can explain why the song is particularly popular within the Beatles catalogue.

Many of the notions within this song are purposefully nonsensical: 'tangerine trees' and 'marmalade skies' are just two examples. The nonsensical nature of the song not only adds to the psychedelic feel it provides, but also encourages imagination from the listener, asking them to partake in the creation of the song's imagery. These notions, of course, tie in to the building blocks of the song, which support the lyrics provided in creating a musical experience unlike any other. It's time for us to take a quick look at the musical aspects of the song that will assist in our exploration of the lyrics themselves.

To create "Lucy in the Sky with Diamonds," a variety of instruments were used: the typical guitar, drums, and vocals played a large part, but instruments like the organ, which played the introductory riff, and the tambura added additional depth to the song. To help with the psychedelic mood of the song, "there is also distorted lead guitar played through a Leslie speaker and an echo effect added to create a surreal and spaced-out feel" (BBC Bitesize, 2021). Another way that the mood of the song is kept consistently is found within the changing of keys within the song, something fairly unusual within Beatles music at this point in their career. The song is played in G sharp major during verses, A major during the pre-chorus, and F sharp major during the chorus itself. As we learned in the introduction to this book, different musical keys have different inherent feelings and meanings: the University of Michigan has notes on these keys and their meanings, which we will explore in relation to "Lucy in the Sky with Diamonds."

G sharp major is a particularly calm key: "everything rustic, idyllic and lyrical, every calm and satisfied passion, every tender gratitude for true friendship and faithful love,--in a word every gentle and peaceful emotion of the heart is correctly expressed by this key" (University of Michigan, n.d.). The fact that the verses are played in this key demonstrates the desire to provide lyrical calmness as the listener imagines floating down the river and includes the visions that Lennon sings to them. The A major key "includes declarations of innocent love, satisfaction with one's state of affairs; hope of seeing one's beloved again when parting; youthful cheerfulness and trust in God" (University of Michigan, n.d.). This key adds to the previous in creating the feeling of innocence and wonder as the listeners continue to float down the river. Finally, the F sharp major key represents "triumph over difficulty, free sigh of relief uttered when hurdles are surmounted; echo of a soul which has fiercely struggled and finally conquered lies in all uses of this key" (University of Michigan, n.d.), which provides additional feelings of glee and relief during the lyrics of the song. Much of the general feeling of this song is provided by the keys themselves and the change in keys, layering feelings upon feelings to create a psychedelic musical experience.

Specific images within the song can be attributed to Lennon, with others brought to life from McCartney's imagination. 'Plasticine porters with looking glass ties' was inspired by a reference to *The Goon Show*, where they discussed 'Plasticine ties,' and was brought to life from Lennon's love for *The Goon Show* (Turner, 2015, p. 181). 'Newspaper taxis' and 'cellophane flowers' were dreamed up by Paul McCartney, whereas John provided the infamous 'kaleidoscope eyes' (Turner, 2015, p. 181). When we connect the lyrics, nonsensical images, and relaxing keys the song is provided in, we emerge with a truly surreal, psychedelic Beatles tune.

"Lucy in the Sky with Diamonds" is so much more than what it is perceived to be. Instead of being a song about drugs and getting high, the song tells a more surreal and psychedelic story inspired by a child's drawing and an image in a children's book. Understanding the story behind the song, the reasons it makes listeners connect and engage with it the way it does, and the story of the real Lucy, provides us with the context to engage with the song on a deeper level and appreciate it for what it truly is: a musical masterpiece.

She's Leaving Home

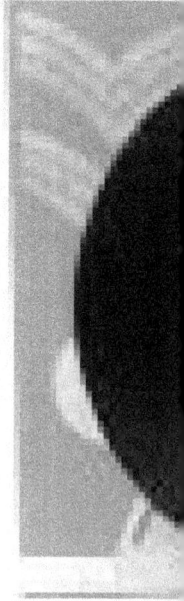

Wednesday morning at five o'clock

As the day begins

Silently closing her bedroom door

Leaving the note that she hoped would say more

She goes down the stairs to the kitchen

Clutching her handkerchief

Quietly turning the backdoor key

Stepping outside, she is free

She, ... (we gave her most of our lives)

Is leaving (sacrificed most of our lives)

Home (we gave her everything money could buy)

Father snores as his wife gets into her dressing gown

Picks up the letter that's lying there

Standing alone at the top of the stairs

She breaks down and cries to her husband

Daddy, our baby's gone.

Why would she treat us so thoughtlessly?

How could she do this to me?

She (we never thought of ourselves)

Is leaving (never a thought for ourselves)

Home (we struggled hard all our lives to get by)

She's leaving home, after living alone, for so many years

Friday morning, at nine o'clock

She is far away

Waiting to keep the appointment she made

Greeting a man from the Motor Trade

She (what did we do that was wrong)

Is Having (we didn't know it was wrong)

Fun (fun is the one thing that money can't buy)

Something inside, that was always denied,

For so many years, .

She's leaving home

Bye bye

'She's Leaving Home' is a particularly poignant Beatles tune for a number of reasons. From its heartfelt story - interestingly enough, based on a true story which was fairly unusual for Beatles songs of this age - to its beautiful orchestration and instrumentation, the song tells an all-too-common story that relates directly to the generational friction existing in the late 1960s. Since there are so many interesting aspects of this song to explore, we will first begin with the story that inspired the song, and then delve into some of the musical decisions that helped create the haunting yet hopeful sound of this memorable Beatles tune.

In February of 1967, the Daily Mail (a favourite newspaper of John Lennon's) printed on the front page, an article about the story of a teenage runaway named Melanie Coe. Coe was described as "a 17-year-old London schoolgirl studying for her A-level GCE exams" (Turner, 2015, p. 186), who had slipped out the door while her parents were away and seemingly vanished. It was her story, written in this newspaper, that inspired Lennon and McCartney to pick up their instruments and share the heartbreaking yet inspiring story of the teenage runaway.

Now, before we go into Melanie's story specifically, let's look at the concept of teenage runaways in the 1960s. As we explored earlier, the 1960s were a tumultuous time of expression, freedom, and radicalism - the 'hippie' counterculture had become extremely popular in younger generations, leaving older generations scratching their heads and trying to find ways to control the explosion of freedom and love that had seemingly taken over the nation. Instead of focusing on building wealth and accepting the materialistic tendencies of the time, the counterculture of the time embraced collectivism and communal living - sharing houses, objects, and in some cases, even toothbrushes. According to Benjamin Ramm, "Between 1967 and 1971, over 500,000 people in the US left home to move into experimental communities" (2017). Many of these people believed in the future: in free love, free thought, and free expression. Benjamin Ramm, BBC writer, continued his explanation of the reasons these people left home by saying that:

For the activists of the New Left, the past was irredeemably tainted by oppressive forces: society has to be reconstructed from the bottom up. The new egalitarian community would be free of hierarchy, patriarchy, racism and the 'false needs' of consumerism and organised religion. The 'replacement society' would eliminate alienation and provide community for young people who, like the teenager in She's Leaving Home, felt they were "living alone for so many years" (2017).

There is an important distinction to make here, in that 'lines between movements were blurry. Many New Leftists were also hippies but not all hippies were consciously supporters of the New Left. Nonetheless, a common denominator was their shared opposition to the war in Vietnam" (Belshaw, 2016). It's also important to note that not every person that ran away during this time period did so to join a counter- or subculture. That being said, there are consistencies in Melanie's story that match with many of the stories of teens that did run away to begin a new way of living.

Melanie's story doesn't quite follow the counterculture story of many of the other individuals her age, but it does follow the story of 'She's Leaving Home' quite closely - more closely than she could have believed, in fact. When interviewed about the song, Melanie said:

> Then there was the line 'after living alone for so many years,' which really struck home to me because I was an only child and I always felt home. [...] I never communicated with either of my parents. It was a constant battle. I left because I couldn't face them any longer (Coe, quoted in Turner, 2015, p. 186).

The generational divide meant that Melanie's parents - her mother in particular - were strict to bringing Melanie up to their beliefs, the beliefs that had driven their generation. It was all about success and money to them, and much like any parent would want for their child, they wanted Melanie to be successful and well-off in her adult life. For Melanie, this meant having her parents control every aspect of her life. "I wasn't allowed

to bring anyone home. She didn't like me going out. I wanted to act,
but she wouldn't let me go to drama school. She wanted me to become
a dentist. She didn't like the way I dressed. She didn't want me to do
anything that I wanted to do" (Coe, quoted in Turner, 2015, p. 187). It was
after this realization that Melanie decided it was finally time: she slipped
out the door one afternoon while her parents were gone, with no intention
of returning. Melanie met with a man named David who worked at a club
she visited, after her departure, and lived with him for a short while until
her parents inevitably caught up with her and took her home.

It wasn't until long after Melanie's escape from her parent's house that she
realized the famous Beatles song was about her. According to a Rolling
Stones interview she did many years later:

> I first heard the song when it came out and I didn't realize it was
> about me, but I remember thinking it could have been about me.
> [...] I found the song to be extremely sad. It obviously struck a
> chord somewhere. It wasn't until later, when I was in my twenties,
> that my mother said, 'You know, that song was about you!' She
> had seen an interview with Paul on television and he said he'd
> based the song on this newspaper article. She put two and two
> together (Runtagh, 2017).

Interestingly, in a strange connection of fate, Melanie had actually met the
Fab Four at an event years before 'She's Leaving Home' was written. On
October 4th, 1963, when she was fourteen years old, Melanie took part
in a lip syncing contest on the program *Ready, Steady, Go* - the Beatles also
happened to be performing for the show that day. Melanie took home first
place in the competition, and her prize was provided to her by none other
than Paul McCartney himself. When asked about this moment,
Melanie said:

> Unfortunately, the moment proved to be somewhat
> underwhelming. "I was very disappointed because there had been
> two shows before mine, and on both of those shows the girl that

won went out on a date with the pop star. I thought I was going to have dinner date with the Beatles, so I was terribly disappointed with my prize!" (Coe, quoted in Runtagh, 2017).

Of course, there was no connection between 'She's Leaving Home' and Melanie's previous encounter with the Beatles, but it is a fascinating coincidence, and makes the story of this song even more intriguing.

Now, there is more to 'She's Leaving Home' than just the fascinating backstory, which means it's time, dear reader, for us to change tactics and move from studying the backstory of the song into studying the song itself. There are three aspects of the song that are worth specific study, as they each play an important and intrinsic part in creating the emotion and energy for the song. First, we will consider the lyrics; in particular, the way in which the lyrics tell two stories. Second, we will consider the connection between the two stories, and the historical musical technique that Lennon and McCartney called upon to make them meaningful. Finally, we will review the instrumentation of the song and why that unique instrumentation provides additional meaning and emotion to this poignant piece.

We've looked at a few of the lyrics in this song already, in relation to Melanie's story, but it's time for us to consider them more in-depth so we can understand how close McCartney's lyrics came to Melanie's story, and where the deviations from her story are, and what they stemmed from. First, let's consider the first few words of the song:

"Wednesday morning at five o'clock
As the day begins [...]"

Whereas Melanie actually left during the afternoon, while her parents were out of the house, McCartney places the unnamed main character of the song as leaving in the early morning. At the time when he wrote the song, McCartney didn't know the intimate details of Melanie Coe's departure, but he did have a reason for the choice of the song beginning with a morning departure. As McCartney explained, the lyrics came to him when he started to write the song: "she slips out and leaves a note and then the parents wake up – It was rather poignant" (McCartney, quoted in Runtagh, 2017). The appeal of the early morning departure spoke to McCartney, as it did to many of his listeners: imagining parents waking up to a note from their child informing them that she had run away creates an impactful and emotional vision.

McCartney artfully continues this emotional scene, when he describes the house after the girl leaves. He focuses in on the mother, who awakens before her husband and finds the note that her daughter has left her:

"[...] Standing alone at the top of the stairs
She breaks down and cries to her husband [...]"

The simple imagery here of a woman standing in her dressing gown, learning that her child has left her, really tugs at one's heartstrings - it's an emotional moment for any listener. The simplicity of the explanation really plays to the listener's favour, because it gives them the opportunity to insert themselves into the song in the way they best understand. Parents might imagine themselves or their partners in the situation of reading the note; children might imagine the devastating impact that a note such as that would have on their parents. If this story was told in a book, for example, there would be far more detail describing the child, the parents, and their relationship, which would make it harder for readers to see themselves within the situation. With less room for detail within the structure of a song, there is more room for interpretation within this medium, leaving the opportunity for listeners to connect more deeply to and imagine more freely scenes like this one.

Now, the other interesting piece of the story that is interesting to note is the detail about why the unnamed girl is leaving home. As we explored earlier, many children who left home at this time did so because they felt too controlled at home. Because of this, they tended to leave to move to communes or communities where more open lifestyles were practiced. It's important to note, then, that the girl in 'She's Leaving Home' doesn't leave for these reasons: she leaves to meet a boy. Beatles songs, and particularly early Beatles songs, tended towards love songs, but this addition is something quite different. Let's consider the lyrics:

"[...] Friday morning, at nine o'clock
She is far away
Waiting to keep the appointment she made
Greeting a man from the Motortrade [...]"

The insinuation here is that the girl ran away from home to be with this boy. Now, interestingly, this was partially the case in Melanie Coe's experience, though it certainly wasn't her only reason for leaving home. There has been discussion, however, about why the Beatles chose this reason for their character to leave home, and further, why she was meeting a man from the MotorTrade. It's been hypothesized that the man from the MotorTrade was an actual person: Terry Doran. Terry Doran and Beatles manager Brian Epstein co-owned Brydor Cars, a luxury car dealership in England. This fact went uncontested for a number of years, but was later denied by Paul McCartney in his biography *Paul McCartney, Many Years from Now*. McCartney stated that:

> "It was just fiction, like the sea captain in 'Yellow Submarine'; they weren't real people. The man from the motor trade was just a typical sleazy character, the kind of guy that could pull a young bird by saying, 'Would you like a ride in my car, darlin'?' Nice plush interior, that's how you pulled birds. So it was just a nice little bit of sleaze" (McCartney, cited in Miles, 1997).

Outside of exploring the lyrics that provide us with imaging and additional stories, we have to also consider the lyrics that change the way in which the story is told. It's time for us to consider the lyrics that contrast the girl's story with the words of her parents. These lyrics occur during three occasions in the song, and provide a glimpse into the way the parents feel about their daughter running away. Before we explore the lyrics themselves, let's explore the way in which they are shared with the audience, because there is a vast and fascinating history behind portraying lines in this way that leads us all the way back to ancient Greece.

One major tradition in Greek theatre was the inclusion of the Greek chorus. Typically, the chorus was a series of actors who wore masks and sang in unison: acting as one character, instead of many. The chorus was more than just a character though:

> The purpose of the Greek chorus was to provide background and summary information to the audience to help them understand what was going on in the performance. They commented on themes, expressed what the main characters couldn't say (like secrets, thoughts, and fears) and provided other characters with information and insights (Hishon, 2016).

In general, the chorus provided context and information that wouldn't typically come out within the natural progression of the story, but was still important for the reader/listener to be aware of. In 'She's Leaving Home,' the equivalent of a Greek chorus is used to provide insight into the parent's feelings about their child running away: their thoughts and emotions that wouldn't typically be able to be expressed within the story and the medium. These lines are sung by John Lennon, making him the equivalent to the chorus if McCartney was the main storyteller. Let's consider the first of three Greek chorus sections:

"[...] She, ... (we gave her most of our lives)
Is leaving (sacrificed most of our lives)
Home (we gave her everything money could buy) [...]"

In opposition to the story McCartney is telling about a girl who feels unloved and disconnected from her parents, Lennon is stepping in to tell the parent's side of the story: how they feel that they have provided everything they possibly can to her parents. In fact, the line 'we gave her everything money could buy' had a strong connection to Melanie Coe's story: she had "two diamond rings, a mink coat, hand-made clothes in silk and cashmere, and even [her] own car" (Turner, 2015, p. 186). Regardless,

Lennon's interjection here demonstrates the pain and betrayal the parents feel upon learning their child is leaving: they have given up their lives to raise her, and provided her with all the material items she could possibly desire. This first chorus demonstrates the shock and lack of understanding as to why their child would leave.

The second chorus, however, tells a bit of a different story, creating a direct disconnect between the main story and the chorus:

" [...] She (we never thought of ourselves)
Is leaving (never a thought for ourselves)
Home (we struggled hard all our lives to get by) [...]"

McCartney weaves a story of a girl who leaves home because she feels as though she's living alone: like her parents are unable to give her a second thought. In the second chorus, Lennon rebuts that theory by expressing the way the parents feel they have never given a thought to themselves; instead, providing everything they can to their child. Interestingly enough, these lines were actually provided by Lennon, and were pulled directly from his childhood. As Jordan Runtagh notes:

> Lennon's contributions were more personal, borrowing scornful lines from his stern Aunt Mimi, who had raised him as a child. "Paul had the basic theme, but all those lines like, 'We sacrificed most of our lives, we gave her everything money could buy, never a thought for ourselves …' those were the things Mimi used to say," he told Hit Parader in 1972. "It was easy to write" (Lennon, quoted in Runtagh, 2017).

This connection to the sacrifices that parents make for their children is easy for parents to relate to, but potentially less easy for children to understand, until they are old enough to make the same sacrifices for the people they care about. Regardless, this addition truly demonstrates the lack of communication between the girl and her parents: one side feels like they are living alone, and the other side feels like they have given up everything to provide the other with a good, happy, comfortable life.

The final chorus provides an even deeper look into the failed relationship between parents and child:

"[...] She (what did we do that was wrong)
Is Having (we didn't know it was wrong)
Fun (fun is the one thing that money can't buy) [...]"

This final chorus demonstrates a shift in thinking for the parents, from not understanding why their child would leave to finally seeing why she elected to move on in her life, away from them. The first two lyrics feel full of self-pity - the parents don't understand what they did wrong, but they never intended to do anything wrong either: all they wanted to do was make a good life for their daughter. The final chorus line demonstrates their understanding that their daughter wants to have fun, and fun was the one thing that they couldn't provide for her with their money. It's a sad and disconcerting understanding, but it ties the story together in the sadness of the parents finally realizing where they had failed their daughter, and why she had chosen to leave them to find the one thing they couldn't provide her with. Though this definitely wasn't the case in the ending of Melanie Coe's story, this ending in 'She's Leaving Home' demonstrates a full circle understanding, albeit with no real resolution, since there is nothing the parents can do to bring their daughter back when the song ends. One of the reasons this song is so impactful is because it provides such a curious ending - satisfying for some, like those who connect with the daughter, and unsatisfying for others, in particular those who connect with the parents.

Outside of the lyrics, there is one additional aspect of this song that we should consider, before completing our analysis: the instrumentation. The Sgt. Pepper era was when the Beatles moved away from their previous touring image and expanded out into new and exciting musical opportunities. Though the Beatles had used orchestral instruments in recordings before this time, noting the unique orchestral makeup for this song will give us an even broader understanding of why this song really tugs at our heartstrings.

For the recording of this song, there were four violins, two violas, two cellos, one double bass, and one harp. Now would be a good time to note that George Harrison and Ringo Starr were not mentioned in the recording whatsoever: this was truly a Lennon/McCartney special. Now, not only is this worth noting: it's also important to recognize that instead of having a baseline provided through the drums or a guitar, in this song, the baseline is provided by the double bass. Now, in order to discuss the instrumentation in this song specifically, we're first going to have to go back in time to review historical purposes and organization of string instruments.

Some of the very first instruments - outside of voices, of course - were stringed instruments. We'll begin our history with the ūd - sometimes known as the Oud - which is a medieval stringed instrument typically used in Muslim music. The ūd doesn't have a standard size or number of strings, but in general:

> The ūd has a deep, pear-shaped body; a fretless fingerboard; and a relatively shorter neck and somewhat less acutely bent-back pegbox than the European lute. The tuning pegs are set in the sides of the pegbox. The gut strings, plucked with a plectrum, are fastened to a tension (guitar-type) bridge on the instrument's belly (Encyclopaedia Britannica, 2021).

The ūd was the precursor, or father to, the lute - a popular stringed instrument in the 16th and 17th centuries that functioned much like the ūd. The lute was similar in many ways to the ūd; in particular, the structure and look of the instrument. Interestingly, the biggest difference between the lute and the ūd is that "European lutes have a large, circular sound hole cut into the belly and ornamented with a perforated rose carved from the belly's wood" (Encyclopaedia Britannica, 2021).

Since the advent and popular use of the lute, its definition has expanded significantly, helped along by its function as the inspiration for many future stringed instruments. Now, the lute is defined as

Any plucked or bowed chordophone whose strings are parallel to its belly, or soundboard, and run along a distinct neck or pole. In this sense, instruments such as the Indian sitar are classified as lutes. The violin and the Indonesian rebab are bowed lutes, and the Japanese samisen and the Western guitar are plucked lutes" (Encyclopaedia Britannica, 2021).

Of course, the history of stringed instruments is not so simple nor compact, but for the purposes of this book, this basic understanding of the movement from the ūd to the lute to the violin is what we need to have in our minds. Now, it's time for us to delve into the stringed instruments present in 'She's Leaving Home.' To begin, let's make sure we all know what the difference is between a violin, viola, cello, and double bass. These instruments all have a rich history, and are typically the first string instruments offered to learners when they begin their music instruction. The biggest differences between the instruments themselves are their size, range, playing position, and their strings. Let's explore these differences to ensure we have a full and accurate understanding of each of these instruments. This understanding will be vital as we explore the reasoning behind using these instruments in this song, and why they make us feel the way they do.

The violin is the smallest of our four instruments, and is played with the musician nestling the violin between their chin and shoulder. Violins have four strings, typically played with musicians pressing down on one or more strings on the neck of the violin as well as bowing or plucking the strings across the bridge. Because it is the smallest instrument in the string family, it has the highest pitch, and is considered a soprano instrument.

The viola is quite similar to the violin, except it is slightly bigger, giving it a lower, alto, tone within the stringed instrument family. It is played in the same way as a violin, and has the same number of strings. Because of its lower tone, it typically plays the harmonies, and it's possible that the viola is one of the first violin family members whose purpose is for accompaniment. That's not to say the viola doesn't get its time in the spotlight: there are a wide variety of well-recognized orchestral pieces that feature the viola.

The cello is substantially different from the violin and viola in structure and how it is played. Though the cello has the same number of strings as the violin and viola, it plays an octave lower than the viola, and instead of being held between the player's chin and shoulder, the cello sits between the players legs and is positioned on the ground using an endpin- not the bottom of the instrument, but a small peg that emerges from the bottom of the instrument that is adjustable to a player's height. There are also many orchestral and solo works that feature the cello.

Finally, the double bass is the lowest pitched string instrument in a typical symphony orchestra, and is structured similarly to the cello - except its players often stand when playing because of the instrument's large size. Typically, double basses are approximately six feet tall. Like all the other instruments we've discussed, the double bass can be seen often in a symphony orchestra, but also in other groups like bluegrass and rock'n'roll as well.

Historically, these instruments were played together as string quartets - sans the double bass, of course. Two violins, a viola, and a cello were put together onstage for string quartets, and they provided beautiful music for any listener. One particular skill of the string quartet, and a skill that is held by all string instruments, is that of evoking emotion from listeners. It has been said that the violin is the saddest instrument of them all, simply because of its ability to bend pitch in a similar way to the human voice. Of course, there is extensive research proving that some of our association with an instrument and an emotion is based on cultural influence: what sorts of music are often played by that instrument factor into how we feel about that instrument. For example, the pipe organ is often connected to sadness and death because culturally, it is associated with funeral processions. Of course, the emotion of an instrument depends on how the instrument is played, the pitch of the song, and many, many more factors - factors we won't delve into at this time.

There are some factors that we will consider in relation to 'She's Leaving Home,' however. First, we'll recognize that the background of string instruments, in lieu of the Beatles' typical guitars, tilts the mood of the song to make it more sombre and low-energy than a typical rock'n'roll tune. Second, we'll also note that the string players aren't always playing their instruments with a bow, as they usually are; instead, in certain places, this song calls for the use of pizzicato strings.

Pizzicato strings refers to a musical technique for playing string instruments where a musician plucks the strings of an instrument instead of using a bow when playing. The result of this technique is a different sound from the instrument: a shorter and sharper sound, when compared to the same note played using a bow. The shorter vibration sounds more direct and piercing, which can cause feelings of tension and discomfort when heard. Of course, as we discussed earlier, these sounds impact different people in different ways based on their cultural upbringing and understanding of the purpose and placement of an instrument, but as a general statement, shorter vibrations as opposed to longer vibrations cause more uncomfortable feelings in listeners. This technique, and its associated feeling, works in favour of 'She's Leaving Home' since the topic of the song is sad and uncomfortable: nobody wants to think about their child running away and leaving them, for any reason. The instrumentation behind the song, and the musical techniques utilized within the song connect to deepen the impact of the lyrics and the way they make their listeners feel.

Our exploration of 'She's Leaving Home' has taken us to many places, some of which we likely didn't expect to consider. If this exploration has proven anything, it's that in terms of Beatles songs, there are no shortages of unexpected yet meaningful connections that their songs draw to the world around us, or around them. Though on the surface, this song appears to be a sad yet surprisingly powerful song about an unloved teen leaving her home, there is actually so much more to the story - not just in terms of the lyrics, but also in terms of the building blocks that make up the song. 'She's Leaving Home' is a true Lennon/McCartney masterpiece that seamlessly weaves truth and fiction together into a beautiful and sad tale that brings the story of a generation to life.

Within You Without You

We were talking about the space between us all

And the people who hide themselves behind a wall of illusion

Never glimpse the truth

Then it's far too late

When they pass away

We were talking about the love we all could share

When we find it, to try our best to hold it there with our love

With our love, we could save the world, if they only knew

Try to realise it's all within yourself

No one else can make you change

And to see you're really only very small

And life flows on within you and without you

We were talking about the love that's gone so cold

And the people who gain the world and lose their soul

They don't know

They can't see

Are you one of them?

When you've seen beyond yourself then you may find

Peace of mind is waiting there

And the time will come when you see we're all one

And life flows on within you and without you

"Within You Without You" is a particularly noteworthy Beatles song for a number of reasons, all of which we will discuss in the coming section. From being the Beatles' second recording in the Indian Classical style to explicitly sharing where future Beatles music was headed, this song was relatively controversial yet has gone down in Beatles history as a turning point in their musical direction, and a notable writing credit for George Harrison. This section will allow us to explore George's history with writing Beatles songs, his interest in Eastern thought, and the background behind "Within You Without You." This discussion, of course, will provide us with the context to properly explore the song's lyrics and deeper meaning.

To begin, let's consider the structure of Beatles songwriting. The vast majority of Beatles songs are attributed to the Lennon/McCartney duo, with substantially less writing credits going to George Harrison and Ringo Starr. That said, George has more writing credits, at 22, than Ringo does at two songs with four additional co-writing credits. Harrison's first writing credit for the Beatles was "Don't Bother Me," included in 1963's record With the Beatles. Interestingly, Harrison felt strongly about the song, but not positively. He believed that: "It's not a very good song, but it at least showed me that, you know, all I needed to do was keep on writing and maybe someday I'd write something good" (Harrison, quoted in Wardle, 2021). Of course, as we well know, Harrison's writing improved exponentially, and he went on to pen some of the most recognizable Beatles hits, including "Something," "Here Comes the Sun," and "While My Guitar Gently Weeps."

When asked about George Harrison's writing for the Beatles, George Martin offered a unique perspective on why it took 'the quiet Beatle' so long to come out of his shell with his songwriting. "George's songwriting was painful for him because he had no one to collaborate with and John and Paul was such a collaborative duo that they would throw out a word of advice to him and so on, but they didn't really work with him" (Martin, quoted in Wardle, 2021). Because George didn't have a collaborator, and because Lennon and McCartney were so used to writing songs in their own way, George was in essence left on his own to figure out the songwriting process from start to finish. As his career grew, of course, he improved, but that does provide an important piece of context for us to consider: much like writing a book, writing a song is an intricate and complex process that can be difficult to do in a bubble without outside input.

"Within You Without You" is one of George's masterpieces, in terms of lyrics, musical structure, and overall vibe and viewpoint. In ways that Lennon and McCartney hadn't managed yet, the song demonstrated the real change between the music the band had previously released and the future of Beatles music. Interestingly enough, when considering how the song represents the philosophical place of the band and the band's future, one of the most fascinating aspects of "Within You Without You" is that George Harrison was the only member of the Beatles who played on the recording. John Lennon was also present for the recording, but left the music up to Harrison, musicians that Harrison had brought on for the recording, and members of the London Symphony Orchestra who played the orchestral parts.

Up until this point in Beatles history, there were very few songs that featured only one of the Beatles. Of course, some quintessential McCartney songs like "Yesterday" and "Blackbird" featured him solo, but this was the first and last Beatles song to feature Harrison without his bandmates. Now, there's likely a few reasons for this; some of them logical, and some of them a bit more personal. For our logical points, let's consider the instrumentation for "Within You Without You." The song didn't feature typical Beatles instruments; instead, it included instruments like the sitar, tambura, swarmandal, and tabla. Harrison played the guitar, sitar, and tambura during the recording, and brought musicians in who knew how to play the other instruments. John, Paul, and Ringo wouldn't have known how to play any of those instruments other than the guitar, so logically, it made sense that they weren't included in the recording. George's vocals were the only vocals required, which meant the other Beatles really had no reason to attend the recording except for support for George, which John provided. The other reasons for the other Beatles not to be included in the recording are a bit more complicated.

In order to truly understand the startings of rifts between members of the Beatles, it's important for us to have the context of where the Beatles were at in terms of their understanding of their music, themselves, and their comfort with drugs at this time in their career. Up until this point, George had been focused very much on his music, but also enjoyed having a good time with his mates. His friends and bandmates noticed a shift in him later on in his career, particularly once he discovered the sitar in 1965, and then began studying a new philosophy. Tony King, a friend of Harrison's, noticed this about him:

> When I first met George in 1963, he was Mr. Fun, Mr. Stay
> Out All Night. Then all of a sudden, he found LSD and Indian
> religion and he became very serious. Things went from rather jolly
> weekends where we'd have steak and kidney pie and sit around
> giggling, to these rather serious weekends where everyone walked
> around blissed out and talked about the meaning of the universe
> (King, quoted in Turner, 2015, p. 193).

Now, George didn't just randomly stumble upon Hinduism and LSD all at the same time; in fact, his story is much more fascinating than that. Let's start with George's history with drugs and LSD, and then move into his religious conversion. In regards to drugs, it's no secret that the Beatles had dabbled in a great many types, and that their drugs of choice impacted their music at different points in their careers. In their early years, even before the Beatles became the Beatles, they were experimenting with drugs like Benzedrine and other stimulants that helped them through the tough, constant, late-night concerts they were performing before their career really took off. The boys were introduced to marijiuana in 1964 by Bob Dylan, after which certain members of the band took a particular liking to the drug. Their enjoyment of pot was quoted as assisting in the creation of *Rubber Soul*, which Lennon has on multiple occasions referred to as the band's pot album. It was, however, their first interaction with LSD that really impacted the band; in particular, Lennon and Harrison.

In the spring of 1965, Lennon, Harrison, and their respective wives drank coffee laced with LSD at the house of John Riley, a dentist. He had put the LSD in their drinks without warning them, though Riley's girlfriend at the time insisted that "John and George had earlier indicated a willingness to take LSD if they didn't know beforehand that it was being administered" (Gilmore, 2016). A recount of their adventure sounds nothing but terrifying: believing there was a fire in the elevator, thinking George's house was a giant submarine, and somehow driving from one place to the other without accident. About the experience, George said: "I had such an overwhelming feeling of well-being, that there was a God, and I could see him in every blade of grass. It was like gaining a hundred years of experience in 12 hours" (Harrison, quoted in Gilmore, 2016).

It was while Harrison was on the set of the second Beatles film *Help!* when he learned about the sitar, a string instrument that originated in medieval India. This was the first opportunity he took to dive in and learn about the instrument and its origins. He taught himself how to play, and used the instrument first on "Norwegian Wood" and then again later in songs like "Within You Without You." His interest in the instrument led him to meet Ravi Shankar, whom Harrison would grow close to in the coming years. Shankar was an Indian musician and composer, who is credited as a huge assistance in popularizing Indian instruments and music in the west during the 1960s and beyond. Harrison and Shankar became close friends, and after the Beatles broke up, toured together and recorded together. To say that Shankar had a huge influence on Harrison is an understatement: Shankar was a huge part of introducing George to Indian music, meditation, and more.

Now, it would be a disservice to our understanding of the Beatles and their connection to Indian music and meditation if we didn't take some time here to explore one of the bigger influences on their music in and around 1968 the Beatles' trip to India. By this point, the band was simply exhausted; after all, it's a lot of work being the Beatles, and keeping up to the world's expectation of the four lads from Liverpool. At this point, the Beatles had stopped touring and had become a studio band, but even then, they were starting to wonder: what's the point in all the riches and fame and fortune? To answer this question, they leaned to the Maharishi Mahesh Yogi. The band had listened to the Maharishi while he was on tour in London in 1967 thanks to Harrison's wife, Pattie Boyd, and in 1968, decided to make a three-month trip to India to meditate, relax, and learn from the Maharishi.

The trip was quite the adventure for the Beatles, as much of the rest of the Beatles' trips were, and resulted in very different learnings for each of the members of the band. George Harrison and John Lennon were the first Beatles to take the trip to India, with McCartney and Starr joining them later on. For Harrison in particular, the trip was like a spiritual awakening, which he took very seriously. When interviewed about the trip, Harrison said that: "the meditation buzz is incredible. I get higher than I ever did with drugs. It's simple ... and it's my way of connecting with God" (Harrison, quoted in Chiu, 2021). He and Lennon were the two that took the trip most seriously, with McCartney and Starr still enjoying themselves - but not necessarily to the same extent. McCartney remembers George's strict focus: "I remember talking about the next album and he would say, 'We're not here to talk to about music – we're here to meditate.' Oh yeah, all right Georgie Boy. Calm down. Sense of humor needed here, you know" (McCartney, quoted in Chiu, 2021).

In fact, Ringo Starr only lasted 10 days at the retreat. Between the bugs, homesickness, and the struggle adapting to the food, he and his wife left soon after their arrival. The trip ended for the other Beatles when a scandal emerged around the Maharishi and he was accused of sexual misconduct. No lawsuits were officially filed against the Maharishi, but the Beatles were quick to distance themselves from the Maharishi in the fallout of the accusation. That said, their time at the retreat was particularly fruitful:

each Beatle had written a variety of songs for upcoming Beatles albums, and the songs that didn't make it onto those albums were featured in their individual works after the Beatles breakup. Their retreat also had a large impact on the way Indian culture and music was adopted in the West: since the Beatles liked it, their fans put an effort into learning about and appreciating it as well.

Though this trip occurred after the release of "Within You Without You," it's important to explore because this song was the first jump that the Beatles took into Indian culture. In fact, though Harrison was brought up as a Roman Catholic, he adopted the Hare Krishna tradition and beliefs until the end of his life. He never fully adopted Hinduism, but he was a particularly religious man, especially after the trip to India in 1968.

Let's take a moment now to consider the way in which "Within You Without You" came to life. According to Tony King:

> Klaus [Voorman] had this pedal harmonium and George went into an adjoining room and started fiddling around on it. It made these terrible groaning noises and, by the end of the evening, he'd worked something out and was starting to sing snatches of it to us. It's interesting that the eventual recording of "Within You Without You" had the same sort of groaning sound that I'd heard on the harmonium because John once told me that the instrument you compose a song on determines the tone of the song" (King, quoted in Turner, 2015, p. 192 - 193).

The focus of the song itself, though, is particularly interesting because it's truly the first opportunity that Harrison took to really express what he'd learned so far about Hindu teachings. Steve Turner explains the song well:

> Written as a remembered conversation, the song put forward the view that individualism - the idea that we each have our own separate identity and existence - is based on an illusion created by the ego and that it encourages disharmony and division. To draw closer to each other and get rid of the "space between us all," we

need to give up this illusion produced by the ego and realize that we are essentially "all one" (Turner, 2015, p. 192).

There are some really raw, meaningful statements within the song that are callouts to actions that we as humans can take to make the world a better place. This is the true story that the song tells: the ways in which we can become better human beings if we can accept that life flows with us and around us; that we are the only ones that can make changes to impact our lives. Of course, this story is told within a fascinating context of Harrison's interest in Indian music and meditation, but also within the varying degrees to which the other members of the Beatles accepted both Harrison's interest and the underlying message within Harrison's studies.

It's time, then, for us to delve into some of the lyrics within this song and dissect their meaning within the context of our previous discussions. The first lyric, in fact, holds meaning in a variety of ways; in particular, the space that was beginning to grow between the Beatles themselves. "We were talking/about the space between us all" provides a bit of a double meaning. On one hand, the line expresses the view that we are all expressly different people, and there is an inherent space between us as individuals, because no two of us are the exact same. On the other hand, the line provides a telling look into the internal workings of the Beatles as a band. Just before the Sgt. Pepper's Lonely Hearts Club Band was recorded, the Beatles took some vacation time separate from each other - freedom that George Harrison really appreciated. Because he appreciated the freedom, it was difficult for him to return to the recordings, and to the same band he'd left, though his views and focus had changed during his time away. He said: "I'd been let out of the confines of the group, and it was difficult for me to come back into the sessions. In a way, it felt like going backwards. Everybody else thought that Sgt. Pepper was a revolutionary record – but for me it was not as enjoyable. I was growing out of that kind of thing" (Harrison, quoted in DeRiso, 2017). This line, then, allows Harrison to speak to the space he felt from his band members; as if he was standing alone instead of alongside his friends and colleagues.

Another line that's worth analyzing is the one whose essence is replicated in the famous "All You Need is Love." As the line in "Within You Without You" goes, "with our love we could save the world." This sentiment was particularly prominent within the next Beatles single, which preached about love being the most important aspect of life. Now, the idea that love can save the world relates to the idea that if people connected with each other's similarities rather than hated and feared each other for their differences, the world would unquestionably become a better place. This belief is held in a variety of philosophies, and connected deeply to Harrison with his newfound focus and philosophical beliefs. Following this line with "if they only knew" likely references his new understanding, and the fact that even though he has this understanding, not everyone else did.

According to Steve Turner, the line "and the people who gain the world/ and lose their soul" has a basis not in Eastern thought, but actually from Jesus and the gospel. He believes that: "the line about gaining the world but losing your soul is taken from a warning given by Jesus and recorded in two of the gospels (Matthew 16 v 26, Mark 8 v 36) (Turner, 2015, p. 192). This line is particularly curious because while the overall song connects intrinsically to the Eastern thought, there are ties to Catholicism, which is how Harrison was brought up. It's possible that this connection was fairly unintentional, but if it was intentional, it's interesting to consider the ways in which Harrison might have meant to demonstrate the similarities between different religions and schools of thought; in a sense, bringing people together through their similarities. If this is intentional, we see Harrison practicing what he preaches, which is meaningful and beautiful all at the same time.

Now, the structure of the song overall is also worth noting, because the song is written as a person remembering a conversation. Much like "Paperback Writer," this choice of song structure is telling in regards to its intention. "Within You Without You" focuses on the idea that we have to connect to each other and realize that we are all one people. By presenting the idea in terms of a conversation, Harrison really drives that point home: the only way we are going to make those connections is by speaking to each other and appreciating our similarities. It's yet another example of the ways in which Harrison practices what he preaches, and it really demonstrates his commitment to sharing his philosophy with the world, but starting with showing his acceptance to the philosophy.

Though "Within You Without You" wasn't the most popular of Beatles songs, there's no question that it provides a unique story about George Harrison, the Beatles and their viewpoints, and the trajectory upon which Harrison's career would move after the Beatles breakup. This song is poignant, meaningful, and quintessentially Harrison: something that wasn't often represented within early Beatles tunes in particular. John Lennon and Ringo Starr both came around to the song later in life, with Lennon referring to it as "one of George's best songs. One of my favorites of his too. He's clear on that song. His mind and his music are clear. There is his innate talent. He brought that sound together" (Lennon, quoted in DeRiso, 2017). This song is a unique blend of past, present, and future, and will forever stand in Beatles history as a supreme George Harrison solo song.

MAGICAL MYSTERY TOUR

I am the Walrus

I am he as you are he as you are me

And we are all together

See how they run like pigs from a gun

See how they fly

I'm crying

Sitting on a corn flake

Waiting for the van to come

Corporation T-shirt, stupid bloody Tuesday

Man you've been a naughty boy

You let your face grow long

I am the egg man

They are the egg men

I am the walrus

Goo goo g'joob

Mister City policeman sitting

Pretty little policemen in a row

See how they fly like Lucy in the sky, see how they run

I'm crying, I'm crying

I'm crying, I'm crying

Yellow matter custard

Dripping from a dead dog's eye

Crabalocker fishwife, pornographic priestess

Boy, you've been a naughty girl, you let your knickers down

I am the egg man

They are the egg men

I am the walrus

Goo goo g'joob

Sitting in an English garden

Waiting for the sun

If the sun don't come you get a tan

From standing in the English rain

I am the egg man (now good sir)

They are the egg men (a poor man, made tame to fortune's blows)

I am the walrus

Goo goo g'joob, goo goo goo g'joob (good pity)

Expert, texpert choking smokers

Don't you think the joker laughs at you (ho ho ho, hee hee hee, hah hah hah)

See how they smile like pigs in a sty, see how they snide

131

I'm crying

Semolina Pilchard

Climbing up the Eiffel tower

Elementary penguin singing Hare Krishna

Man, you should have seen them kicking Edgar Allen Poe

I am the egg man

They are the egg men

I am the walrus

Goo goo g'joob, goo goo goo g'joob

Goo goo g'joob, goo goo goo g'joob, goo

Joob, joob, jooba

Jooba, jooba, jooba

Joob, jooba

Joob, jooba

Umpa, umpa, stick it up your jumper (jooba, jooba)

Umpa, umpa, stick it up your jumper

Everybody's got one (umpa, umpa)

Everybody's got one (stick it up your jumper)

Everybody's got one (umpa, umpa)

Everybody's got one (stick it up your jumper)

Everybody's got one (umpa, umpa)

Everybody's got one (stick it up your jumper)

Everybody's got one (umpa, umpa)

Everybody's got one (stick it up your jumper)

Everybody's got one (umpa, umpa)

Everybody's got one (stick it up your jumper)

Everybody's got one (umpa, umpa)

[Extract from pre-recorded scene from Shakespeare's *King Lear*, Act 4, Scene 6]:

Slave

Thou hast slain me

Villain, take my purse

If I ever

Bury my body

The letters which though find'st about me

To Edmund Earl of Gloucester

Seek him out upon the British Party

O untimely death

I know thee well

A serviceable villain, as duteous to the vices of thy mistress

As badness would desire

What, is is he dead?

Sit you down, Father, rest you

"I am the Walrus" is a well-recognized song by most Beatles fans, and it's well known for its confusing and fairly disjointed nature. For many a year, fans have poured over this song in attempts to find out exactly what was going through John Lennon's mind as he was writing it; when we consider its curious lyrics, it's not difficult to understand just how much of a task that would be. This provides us, dear readers, the opportunity to explore the context behind the song, as well as the song itself, to help understand some of the interesting concepts within the song. In particular, we'll discuss how the song ties into the 'Paul is Dead' conspiracy theory and exactly what inspired John Lennon to write this fascinating tune.

To begin, let's discuss the elephant (or the eggman) in the room: this song makes very little sense. Partly, this fact can be attributed to the reality that "I am the Walrus" resulted from the connection of three songs that John had been working on at the time: "the first, inspired by hearing a distant police siren while at home in Weybridge, started with the words 'Mis-ter c-ity police-man' and fitted the rhythm of the siren. The second was a pastoral melody about his Weybridge garden. The third was a piece of nonsense about sitting on a cornflake" (Turner, 2015, p. 220). After reading these original ideas and thinking about the resulting song, it's not difficult to understand exactly how convoluted and confusing "I am the Walrus" is. Interestingly enough, confusion was actually John Lennon's purpose for the song.

As it turns out, just before writing this song, Lennon received a letter from a student who was analyzing the contents of Beatles songs for a class:

> The catalyst was a letter received from a pupil of Quarry Bank School, which mentioned that an English master was getting his class to analyse Beatles' songs. This was sent to John by Steven Baley [...]. The idea of Beatles' songs being analyzed as part of a literature course in his old school amused John, who decided to confuse such students by writing a song full of the most perplexing and incoherent clues (Turner, 2015, p. 220).

With this in mind, the fact that "I am the Walrus" is confusing actually makes sense: it's purpose was to confuse the people that attempted to understand its deeper meaning. This sort of decision - to create unrealistic and perplexing images for an audience - wasn't unknown for Lennon; in fact, it tied back to some writing that he had done in his early life. His book *In His Own Write* has been compared to "I am the Walrus" in that the nonsense stories and poems present in the book were a precursor to songs like the one at hand. Lennon was inspired by many writers, but in particular, Lewis Carroll, writer of *Alice in Wonderland*. This fact tightens our understanding of Lennon's style even further, because Carroll's writing included some fairly nonsensical and occasionally dark ideas. Not only that: Lennon's writing has been positively compared to that of James Joyce, though Lennon didn't actually know who Joyce was at the time. For the purposes of really understanding the connection between Lennon's early writings and "I am the Walrus," let's explore a short excerpt from *In His Own Write*.

"I'm a moldy moldy man
I'm moldy thru and thru
I'm a moldy moldy man
You would not think it true
I'm moldy til my eyeballs
I'm moldy til my toe
I will not dance I shyballs
I'm such a humble Joe" (Lennon, quoted in Goodreads, 2021).

In His Own Write was released during the height of Beatlemania, and sold remarkably well. The book was helpful in cementing John in his role of 'the smart Beatle.' Of course, his role in both Beatles films, as well as being half of the Beatles songwriting duo assisted in keeping up that image for him as well. Part of this charm of Lennon's was managing to mix nonsense with genuine logic and smarts: something that he accomplished well within "I am the Walrus." Before we jump into an exploration of the lyrics themselves, we have a few more aspects of the overall song to explore. Let's look at the building blocks of the song to help further our understanding of its unique composition.

Musicologist Alan Pollack explored the musical aspects of "I am the Walrus" and established some interesting facts about the arrangement of the song. The song is written in the A-major key, which according to the University of Michigan, "includes declarations of innocent love, satisfaction with one's state of affairs; hope of seeing one's beloved again when parting; youthful cheerfulness and trust in God" (n.d.). In some ways, this fits with the theme of the song, because it's intended as a cheery, teasing song, and if we could be so bold, the song likely gave John Lennon immense satisfaction to consider the people - much like the authors of this book - that would research and agonize over finding the deeper meaning within this song when he intended that none exist. That said, the authors of this book make a strong argument that the simple fact that the song was written with the intention of creating confusion makes the song worth exploring, because it's important to explore the story behind the song, and the ways in which Lennon attempted to tie together concepts that had no intellectual value nor purpose.

It's important to note, then, that when Alan Pollack looked deeper than the lyrics, he found some quintessential Beatles-isms:

> Many times I've told you how wherever you find the Beatles at their most far out you also find them, under the surface, operating on their most classical instincts. So don't be fooled here: no matter what else you may respond to in this wonderfully outrageous song, you should acknowledge the extent to which it ultimately weighs in as a (granted, extremely stylized and abstract) talkin' blues number (Pollack, n.d.).

Even though the song seems chaotic in its structure, Pollack found a musical connection that ties back to some of the Beatles' original tunes, such as "I Should Have Known Better" and "Thank You Girl." At this point in the Beatles' career, they were still experimenting with new musical opportunities, and though they did have some songs that branched out drastically from their early tunes, it is songs like "I am the Walrus" that truly demonstrated the Beatles' maintained connection to their early roots.

Much like "A Day in the Life," "I am the Walrus" utilized much more than just the Beatles, their guitars, and their drums. In fact, "the recording of "I am the Walrus" began on September 5. It lasted on and off throughout the month because George Martin was trying to find an equivalent to the flow of images and wordplay in the lyrics by using violins, cellos, horns, clarinet and a 16-voice choir, in addition to the Beatles themselves" (Turner, 2015, p. 221). The complicated nature of the song meant that the music itself was difficult to put together in a way that properly represented the song, its vibe, and its lyrics. Of course, George Martin was considered the Fifth Beatle because of the amount of time he spent working for the group, so he was uniquely positioned to not only know exactly what John Lennon was looking for, but also know how to bring that vision to life.

In the end, Alan Pollack described the orchestration thusly:

> The overall effect of the orchestration is surreal in a manner analogous to that of a colorized classic film. The overlay of orchestra and chorus underscores various details of imagery in the words and music with exaggerated gestures suggestive of some crazy cartoon soundtrack; e.g. stumbling triplets after "see how they run," the glissandi behind "crying," the laughing at the choking smokers, and the "sneiding" pigs. Glissandi, by the way, serve an almost leitmotific role in their constant reappearance at different places and in different speeds (n.d.).

Now, let's take some time to explore the lyrics of the song: which are nonsense, which are logical, and which land somewhere in-between. The first line of the song "I am he as you are me/and we are all together" is one of the more sensible and serious lines within the song: though that's contested between scholars and John Lennon. Scholars believed that the opening line represented "a paraphrase of the quote by the spiritual teacher Gurdjieff: 'I am Thou. Thou art I. He is Ours. We both are His'" (Turner, 2015, p. 221). Lennon, on the other hand, suggested it was the result of an acid trip. In one of his final interviews before his untimely death, Lennon said this about "I am the Walrus;"

> The first line was written on one acid trip one weekend. The second line was written on the next acid trip the next weekend, and it was filled in after I met Yoko ... I'd seen Allen Ginsberg and some other people who liked Dylan and Jesus going on about Hare Krishna. It was Ginsberg, in particular, I was referring to. The words 'Element'ry penguin' meant that it's naïve to just go around chanting Hare Krishna or putting all your faith in one idol. In those days I was writing obscurely, à la Dylan. [...] It never dawned on me that Lewis Carroll was commenting on the capitalist system. I never went into that bit about what he really meant, like people are doing with the Beatles' work. Later, I went back and looked at it and realized that the walrus was the bad guy in the story and the carpenter was the good guy. I thought, Oh, shit, I picked the wrong guy. I should have said, 'I am the carpenter.' But that wouldn't have been the same, would it? [Sings, laughing] 'I am the carpenter ...' (Lennon, quoted in Sheff, 2000).

Of course, there's no argument that the song sounds like it was created in a drug-induced haze, but it is interesting (and likely would be entertaining to Lennon himself) that scholars have managed to extract meaning from the song even though it was intended to be meaningless - and even more interesting that the lyric in question was one that Lennon confirmed he had written while on an acid trip. One of the reasons the authors elected to include an analysis of this song within this book was so that we had the opportunity to explore a clear case of intent of the songwriter versus analysis of the general public. It's also entirely possible that there are meanings existing within the song that Lennon included unintentionally; after all, it sounds like his songwriting process wasn't the most sober of occasions.

This does bring a curious notion to mind, though, when considering the song itself. If we think back to "Lucy in the Sky with Diamonds," we will remember that the song was believed to be about drugs, when Lennon insisted that it was intended as nothing more than a song about a drawing by his son. There are hints that, though it's fairly clear to listeners that "I am the Walrus" was written while Lennon was on drugs, the song might actually hide some references to drugs and drug usage. As Jon Wiener notes in his essay *Sgt. Pepper and the Flower Power:*

> The first line referred to the LSD-inspired project of destroying his ego - "I am he as you are he" - and asserted the Sixties communal ideal: 'we are all together.' In each verse, John poured out a torrent of disjointed images, ending with 'I'm crying.' He sang that line without expression, with a blankness that was frightening. He was hinting that LSD wasn't working for him, but he was also disguising his bad feelings in a dizzying spectacle of sounds and words, as he had done with 'Strawberry Fields Forever.' He was not yet able to tell the truth simply and directly (Wiener, 2004).

As we Beatles fans are well aware, Lennon did reach a point in his writing wherein he was able to express his truth without shame, but for the most part, those songs didn't exist until after the Beatles broke up. At this point in his songwriting career, Lennon was still finding ways to quietly cry out for help, but cover his pain with other means, much like he did with the band's hit "Help!" This fact ties back to the interesting dichotomy between the intent of the song and the song itself: even though it was intended to be meaningless, the simple act of making the song meaningless inherently provided it with meaning.

All that said, there are other lyrics that are worth analyzing: to see what the stories behind them are believed to be. For example, we will look in detail at the identity of the walrus when we explore the meaning behind "Glass Onion," but when the song came out, Lennon admitted he had not actually written the song knowing who the eggman and the walrus were. That said, fans of the "Paul is Dead" conspiracy theory believed that another clue in the ongoing puzzle was that Paul was the walrus, and that was a part of proving his death. This concept was directly referenced in "Glass Onion," which we will discuss in a later section. There were also, however, other characters within the song that Beatles scholars believe were based on actual people - intentionally or not.

Not only was the discussion of the walrus's identity one of great contention - debate swirled around who the eggman was. It's believed that: "the 'eggman' supposedly referred to the Animals' vocalist Eric Burdon, who had an unusual practice of breaking eggs over his female conquests while making love and became known amongst his musical colleagues as 'the egg man'" (Turner, 2015, p. 221). In fact, it seems that 'the egg man' was a running joke between Burdon and Lennon, as Burdon confirmed in a later interview:

> It may have been one of my more dubious distinctions, but I was the Eggman — or, as some of my pals called me, 'Eggs,'" writes Burdon. It all started one sunny morning when he stood in the kitchen, "cooking breakfast naked except for my socks," and a "Jamaican girlfriend called Sylvia" took it upon herself to send the meal in an entirely different direction. She slid up beside me and slipped an amyl nitrate capsule under my nose. As the fumes set my brain alight and I slid to the kitchen floor, she reached to the counter and grabbed an egg, which she cracked into the pit of my belly (Burdon, quoted in Giles, 2015).

It's unsurprising that a story of this nature would entertain John Lennon, who then included the phrase 'eggman' in "I am the Walrus." Whether it was intentionally a reference to Burdon or simply an idea brought on with the help of some psychedelic drugs we will never know, but it does provide an interesting story to tell the next time "I am the Walrus" plays at a party.

There's yet another character worth analyzing within "I am the Walrus," yet it's a character that is not well known: semolina pilchard. According to popular singer Marianne Faithfull, certain wording within the song leads to the belief that semolina pilchard represents Detective Sergeant Norman Pilcher, "the Metropolitan police officer who gained a reputation for targeting pop stars (including John) for drug possession" (Turner, 2015, p. 220). Before we jump into the lyrics and wording that led to the equating of Pilcher with semolina pilchard, let's explore Pilcher's history, particularly as it relates to John Lennon.

As journalist Duncan Campbell notes, "Pilcher was famous in the 1960s. He felt the velvet collars of the era's best-known rock stars and was responsible for some of its highest-profile arrests. But the squad he worked for was riddled with corruption and Pilcher himself ended up behind bars for four years for perjury" (2020). Pilcher's name was associated with high profile arrests including Dusty Springfield, Brain Jones, George Harrison, and Levi Stubbs. It was reported that these celebrities were targeted by Pilcher specifically, but Pilcher maintains that: "he himself, like so many of the drug squad's targets at the time, was the victim of a stitch-up" (Campbell, 2020). It did appear that in the case of John Lennon, Pilcher was a bit of a fan. About Lennon, Pilcher said: "His ideas of peace and kindness were expressed in his demeanour and attitude, which was quite humbling indeed" (Pilcher, quoted in Campbell, 2020). That said, Pilcher also got to see Lennon's more sarcastic side: when Lennon was in Japan, he sent Pilcher a postcard "with the greeting, 'you can't get me now!'" (Campbell, 2020).

Of course, the lyrical connection between Pilcher and pilchard makes the most sense in terms of connecting the man and the lyric together. At the same time, though, there were also lyrical clues that tied into the story. "Sitting on a cornflake/waiting for the van to come" could refer to Lennon's knowledge that Pilcher was on his tail, and Lennon waiting for the day that Pilcher would catch him. That said the original line was actually 'waiting for the man to come'; interestingly, Hunter Davies misheard Lennon's original lyric, and Lennon liked it so much that he decided to change it. With that in mind, it's interesting to note the way in which Pilcher found Lennon, the day he finally arrested him. "On 18

October 1968, wearing a postman's hat as a disguise, Pilcher led the squad as they crashed into the Marylebone flat of John Lennon and Yoko Ono and discovered that "they were stark naked!"" (Campbell, 2020). However, this arrest occurred after the release of "I am the Walrus," so whether it was Lennon's intention or not is up for debate.

Regardless of Lennon's intentions with the line 'semolina pilchard,' the perceived connection to Norman Pilcher is a fascinating story, and not actually too difficult to see within the context of the song. Though we will never really know if, in a moment of genius, Lennon had informed everyone that there wasn't any meaning to "I am the Walrus," yet left select clues anyway just to watch Beatles fans consider and reconsider the lyrics and what they meant, we do know that "I am the Walrus" is a one-in-a-million song whose confusing genius can't be replicated.

On a final note, let's remember the fact that when Lennon finished writing "I am the Walrus," his response to friend Pete Shotton was "let the fuckers work that one out" (Lennon, quoted in Turner, 2015, p. 221).

Rocky Raccoon

The BEATLES

Now somewhere in the black mining hills of Dakota

There lived a young boy named Rocky Raccoon

And one day his woman ran off with another guy

Hit young Rocky in the eye

Rocky didn't like that

He said, "I'm gonna get that boy"

So one day he walked into town

Booked himself a room in the local saloon

And Rocky Raccoon checked into his room

Only to find Gideon's bible

But Rocky had come equipped with a gun

To shoot off the legs of his rival

His Rival it seems had broken his dreams

By stealing the girl of his fancy

Her name was Magill, and she called herself Lil

But everyone knew her as Nancy

Now, she and her man, who called himself Dan

Were in the next room at the hoe-down

And Rocky burst in, and grinning a grin

He said, "Danny boy, this is a showdown"

But Daniel was hot, he drew first and shot

And Rocky collapsed in the corner

Now the doctor came in stinking of gin

And proceeded to lie on the table

He said, "Rocky, you met you match"

And Rocky said, "Doc, it's only a scratch

And I'll be better, I'll be better, Doc, as soon as I am able"

And now Rocky Raccoon, he fell back in his room

Only to find Gideon's bible

Gideon checked out, and he left it no doubt

To help with good Rocky's revival

C'mon, Rocky boy

C'mon, Rocky boy

At first glance "Rocky Raccoon" doesn't stand out in the realm of Beatles songs, and you won't find it on any greatest hit compilations. While it isn't as well revered as some other tracks off of the Beatles eponymous album *The Beatles*, also known as the *White Album*, it is definitely not a track to be scoffed at. While it may be waved away as simple, it is a track that holds its own charm for many fans. It begins by introducing the audience to it's protagonist, Rocky Raccoon, a young boy who lives in the hills of Dakota. Which Dakota? Well with the descriptor of "black mining hills" we can deduce that the song must take place in the Black Hills of South Dakota. Now that we know that this story takes place in a place known for its mining, we can picture the type of rough and tumble folks who could live there, with Rocky being one of them. This note gives the listener a clearer picture of its characters. As the song continues we can learn that Rocky is upset because his girlfriend has run off with another man who also happened to give Rocky a black eye. Rocky, fueled with anger, sets out for revenge.

" [...] Booked himself a room in the local saloon

And Rocky Raccoon checked into his room

Only to find Gideon's bible

But Rocky had come equipped with a gun

To shoot off the legs of his rival [...]"

Once he gets to town he checks himself into a room at the saloon where he finds a Gideon's bible, which is not a special kind of bible, rather a free bible that is distributed by The Gideons International association. This bible is placed here to set up the hint of a redemption for Rocky at the end of the story. It is for the same reason that the mention of Gideon's bible here is paired with the fact that Rocky had come with a gun to fulfill his revenge with devastating violence. The next time Gideon's bible is mentioned, it will come under very different circumstances. The song then introduces the name's of the two people that Rocky is pursuing -- His girlfriend Magill, or Lil who is known to everyone else by the name of Nancy, and Dan, the man who she ran away with. Rocky bursts into the hoedown taking place next door to confront Dan and Nancy proclaiming to Dan that "this is a showdown" and the fight begins. Unfortunately for Rocky, he is once again bested by Dan who has the quicker hand. The doctor, possibly drunk off of the gin that he stinks of, proclaims that he is unsure of Rocky's chances, while Rocky waves him off by telling him his injuries are only a scratch and nothing to worry about.

"[...]And now Rocky Raccoon, he fell back in his room

Only to find Gideon's bible

Gideon checked out, and he left it no doubt

To help with good Rocky's revival[...]"

In this set of lyrics leading to the end of the song we can see Gideon's bible is brought up once again but as mentioned before in much different circumstances. Rocky, having lost not only his pride and will for revenge but also some blood, now resides on his bed hoping that he heals soon. Rocky, seeing the bible, seems to mistake Gideon as a former resident of the room who left it there. The last line implies a sort of redemption for Rocky, as he hopes that it will help with his revival. The audience is left to wonder how Rocky made out, if he lived or not, and if he gained the redemption he was seeking in our final moments with him.

While it may be easy to write "Rocky Raccoon" off as a simple story with straight forward musical backing that would be selling the song short. It is a track that encapsulates the group's fun and creativity in writing songs on an album that is primarily focused on just that. While *The Beatles* may not hold the same adventurous feelings or growth in musical qualities as the preceding albums, it holds a particular charm throughout it's runtime. It is not an album focused on pushing the boundaries of rock and roll, rather a love letter to the music that influenced them and a conscious effort to make music for the sake of making music. Carl Belz makes this a point when discussing the sometimes controversial album, stating:

> "I want to argue that the Beatles' return to the past is neither a 'put-down' nor a 'put-on', but an expression of consciousness which is unprecedented in the history of rock and which defines the 1968 album as fine art. Specifically, it is a consciousness of the fact that the record is, after all, a record. That is, the album is non-metaphoric: Its primary purpose is not to talk about the world, create pictures of it, or refer to specific experiences with it. The primary purpose of *The Beatles* is to present a conscious experience of music as music." (Belz, 1969/2009)

"Rocky Raccoon," originally Rocky Sassoon during the writing process (Turner, 2015, p. 246), is one of many songs on *The Beatles* that showcases the group's exploration of storytelling through songwriting. Many of the Beatles' early tracks allow the listener to insert themselves into the lyrics, whether it be a song about love or one about heartbreak. However, this song features a protagonist and an antagonist along with a proper story structure and a narrator recounting the story, possibly someone who could have been close to the characters within the song. With *The Beatles* being a love letter to the music that the group loved, it would be amiss to ignore the influences that they feature in "Rocky Raccoon." The lyrics of the song harken to classic outlaw country and folk ballads you might hear from Marty Robbin's "Gunslinger Ballads and Trail Songs" and a style of musical storytelling that would only become more popular into the 1970's and 80's through an influx of Outlaw Country with artists such as Willie Nelson and Waylon Jennings leading the charge. The song could also be a spoof on classic American folk ballads, playing on folk ballad parodies of the past from artists such as Bob Dylan (Price, 1997). Another possible influence may be Robert W. Services' poem "The Shooting of Dan McGrew" where two characters fight over their supposed sweetheart (Turner, 2015, p. 246). Both "Rocky Raccoon" and Services' poem feature a character named "Dan" as one of the men fighting for their love.

The structure of the song's third person narrator as well as the protagonists' struggles are not the only parallels that "Rocky Raccoon" share with other country outlaw and folk ballad stories. The Gideon's Bible in Rocky's room at the saloon is also another inclusion familiar to the genre, as religion is commonly a large theme within outlaw country songs where the protagonist seeks some form of redemption or transcendence (Fraser, 2018). The narrator hints at Rocky seeking religious redemption at the end of the song, where while lying on his bed he finds Gideon's bible once again and it is suggested that the book was left by Gideon to help with Rocky's revival. An interpretation of this line may suggest that the bible will not only be a part of Rocky's physical healing process, but his spiritual one as well. This also contrasts the first account of the bible in Rocky's room, where he seemingly ignores it as his sole purpose for being there is to act on the revenge he seeks against Dan. Gideon's bible plays a huge role in Rocky's journey, from a man set on retribution against the man who took the love of his life, to one who now is searching for physical and spiritual healing in the aftermath of his devastating loss.

In terms of the song's musical structure, it seems standard on the surface, being in the Key of C Major and 4/4 time. However, where this song's structure is deceptively interesting is in how it keeps the listeners attention. "Rocky Raccoon" features an unwavering eight-bar chord progression that plays over and over. While this may get tiring to a listener's ear after the 3 minute and 33 second runtime of the track, what keeps it fresh is McCartney's vocal style, the storytelling lyrics, and the group's instrumentation (Pollack, 1998).

The post-1965 Beatles became more focused on their lyrics as they believed that their work up to that point was shallow and simple (MacDonald, 2007). With this shift in mindset the group began exploring their lyrical songwriting more in depth, and in turn displaying their charm and wit through their songs. "Rocky Raccoon," being a parody of classic American storytelling and musical tropes, showcases the Beatles brand of humor and their explorations of that humor through their songs. This can most easily be heard in McCartney's delivery of the first verse, where he employs a faux American accent. When asked about the accent in an interview, McCartney stated.

> "Oh that. Yeah, that was just a joke, you know, as most of it is" (McCartney, cited in Macurthur, 1968).

McCartney and the rest of the group's willingness to cast aside a more serious approach of songwriting to encourage creativity in storytelling is a definite mark of the Beatles late career. Their creativity also shines through in the playful bridge sections of the song, where a ragtime type of piano piece is played while McCartney vocalizes a melody over top with non-lexical vocables. This focus on being humorous and at times even goofy in the writing of the songs as well as the performance of it contrasts with the song's lyrics, which include more serious themes of revenge and redemption. The mix of humor and seriousness is not all too strange when discussing McCartney's songwriting. Not even a year later another song that features this dichotomy in songwriting, "Maxwell's Silver Hammer", would make its way onto *Abbey Road.*

The instrumentation of the song takes familiar sounds from famous American genres such as Rock and Roll, Folk and country. The constant strumming of an acoustic guitar plays through the song and during the verse is only accompanied with McCartney's vocal delivery and the occasional wailing of a harmonica, an instrument very prominent in American folk music. The harmonica is not a strange instrument to hear in Beatles songs either, having made appearances on early tracks such as "Love Me Do." Electric instruments such as electric guitar and bass as well as drums slowly and subtly introduce themselves into the song. The last instrument that makes an appearance is the honky tonk style piano that plays during the bridge and the ending of the song. Leading up to the end portion of the song, just after Gideon's bible is mentioned for the second time, the very familiar effect of the Beatles vocal harmonies is used to invoke the idea of a church choir as Rocky begins his journey of redemption.

But does "Rocky Raccoon" have any reverence in popular culture? Again, while it is not one of the Beatles most popular songs it can be linked to significant and sadly dark events as this track does appear on *The Beatles*, an album connected with the Manson murders. While "Helter Skelter" is the most famously connected track with the group's atrocities, and a title we will discuss later in this book, the entirety of *The Beatles* influenced them in one way or another. "Rocky Raccoon" may contain no direct reference to race or war to any well-adjusted human being, but Manson found a way to link it into his sick theories. To Manson the use of the word "raccoon" was meant to represent Black Americans as it was also used as a derogatory term for black men (Felton & Dalton, 1970). On a happier note, the song is possibly the inspiration for the name of Rocket Raccoon, a Marvel character popularized to much of the world through his inclusion in the Guardians of the Galaxy comics and films (Collins, 2014). The Marvel character's rough and tumble attitude and his hunger for combat may also show that Rocket and Rocky share more similarities than just their namesake. While the song may not be top of mind for many Beatles fans, a character like Rocket Raccoon's ascent to pop culture icon in the 2010's shows that the legacy of the Beatles can live on outside of their music through the inspiration they have given others.

The track's legacy is indeed difficult and inspiring all at once. From the darkest depths of humanity's depravity to the highest reaches of our imaginations, "Rocky Raccoon" has it all covered. However, this legacy that others have built for it may be fitting. Though it is ultimately a song about the darkness that inhabits all human beings and the redemption one can seek, it is paired with a structure inherited from American gunslinger ballads brought about from the Beatles' open creative process. The legacy of this song is not always one that is easy to look at, but is one that in some ways is reaffirmed by the track itself: a legacy of the evil and good of humanity not always at odds or related with one another, but rather coexisting in an ever-changing world.

Blackbird

The BEATLES

Blackbird singing in the dead of night

Take these broken wings and learn to fly

All your life

You were only waiting for this moment to arise

Blackbird singing in the dead of night

Take these sunken eyes and learn to see

All your life

You were only waiting for this moment to be free

Blackbird fly, blackbird fly

Into the light of a dark black night

Blackbird fly, blackbird fly

Into the light of a dark black night

Blackbird singing in the dead of night

Take these broken wings and learn to fly

All your life

You were only waiting for this moment to arise

You were only waiting for this moment to arise

You were only waiting for this moment to arise

'Blackbird' is one of Paul McCartney's most recognized songs – both within the Beatles and throughout his solo career. This song is credited to the Lennon/McCartney songwriting duo, but in reality the majority of the work for this song was done by McCartney himself. 'Blackbird' is a particularly interesting Beatles song not only because there are a variety of disputed stories surrounding its technical intent, but also because one of those stories, confirmed in part by McCartney, takes on a topic much heavier than any other Beatles tune to date. Of course – intent of the song aside – the song is a beautiful one, sharing images of a blackbird with broken wings regaining flight, but the song is made even more meaningful when one is aware of the true meaning behind the haunting tune.

The first question that arises when considering the meaning of 'Blackbird' regards when the tune was actually written. The song was written in 1968, but as Steve Turner notes, "the exact month is difficult to pinpoint since Paul has said he wrote it not in India but on his Scottish farm. It's possible that he started the music in India, influenced by Donovan, and completed the song between his return to England on March 26 and the demo recordings at George's Esher home in late May" (2015, p. 245). Now, reader, you may be wondering why it is important when McCartney actually wrote the lyrics to this song. As was previously mentioned, there are multiple stories surrounding the meaning of 'Blackbird,' one of them dependent on the time at which the lyrics were written. Let's jump into some of the stories behind the song; as we do so, we'll explore how the lyrics can be interpreted based on each story.

Before we explore the stories themselves, we need to understand why the timing of the song is particularly important: when it was written plays a huge impact on the perceptions surrounding the song's meaning. Many people connect the song to the civil rights movement happening in the United States at the time, and view the song as a message of support to black activists who were 'taking their broken wings and learning to fly.' We will explore this story in more detail later on in this section, especially since "close to the time of recording [McCartney] never mentioned the connection with America's racial strife" (Turner, 2015, p. 245). In fact, in an early interview, McCartney stated that "there's nothing to the song. It's just one of those 'pick it and sing it' [songs] and that's it" (McCartney, quoted in Turner, 2015, p. 245).

The speculation surrounding the time in which the song was written ties in closely with what was occurring in the United States at the time, because if McCartney finished the song between March and May of 1968, then the likelihood is that it was completed after the assassination of Martin Luther King Jr on April 4, 1968. Martin Luther King Jr was an outspoken advocate for equal rights in America, and his death sparked another fire in the fight for equal rights, returning the topic to news outlets across the globe. It was likely through these outlets that McCartney began to read about the topic, and decided to use his song to share a message of hope to the people who needed it.

With the time of the writing of the song in mind, we can now move forward to explore some of the many stories that surround the infamous Beatles song. According to Paul's step mother, Angie, the song was written for her mother, whose name was Edie. As her story goes, Paul visited Edie before her death, and Edie told him of a blackbird that would sing outside her window, inspiring McCartney to record the sound of the bird and use it in his song. This story is corroborated, in part, by the fact that Angie has "a copy of the studio take where Paul says 'This one's for Edie' before recording it" (Turner, 2015, p. 245). That said, this story hasn't taken off much because of the strength of some of the other stories, which we will soon explore. At the same time, it's entirely possible that McCartney felt inspired by Edie's story, and did dedicate one of the recordings to her as a thanks for providing him the inspiration to use a blackbird as an image within a song.

Now, early on after "Blackbird" was written, McCartney said "that the tune was inspired not by a blackbird's singing but by Bach's 'Bouree in E Minor' (from the lute suite 'BWV 996) that he had learned as a teenager from a guitar manual" (Turner, 2015, p. 245). According to this story, McCartney had never quite been able to play Bach's tune correctly, and when he attempted to play it, the tune that became "Blackbird" was what came out. The words, of course, were a much different matter, and they are going to make up the bulk of our analysis, as it's the intended meaning behind them that demonstrates the true power of this song.

Let's look, then, at the title of the song and it's etymology. This analysis will prove particularly interesting, as it will allow us to properly understand the connotations behind the term 'blackbird' and any of the meanings that have seeped their way into the song. In the most literal of senses, the term blackbird refers to a bird with black feathers; in particular, a common European thrush. Male thrushes are black with yellow beaks, hence calling them blackbirds. If we dive a bit deeper into the etymology of the phrase blackbird, we find a more sinister meaning. Various dictionaries list a definition of blackbird as "(formerly) a person, especially a Pacific Islander, who was kidnapped and sold into slavery abroad" (Dictionary.com, 2021). Similarly, if the phrase 'blackbirding' is used as a verb, it means "to kidnap (a person)" (Dictionary.com, 2021). Blackbirding was, unfortunately, a fairly common practice and didn't truly die out until the early 1900s when legislation was put in place by the Australian Commonwealth.

In addition, as Steve Turner explains, "the use of the term 'blackbird' to refer to people of African origin dates back to the slave trade wand was always used pejoratively" (Turner, 2015, p. 245). It is more likely that McCartney knew about the use of the phrase in regards to people of African origin, and not so much of its less recent history referring to Pacific Islanders. That said, the etymology of the word says everything it needs to: there is a strong tie connecting the phrase 'backbird' to the slave trade and to the struggle of surpression in America and across the globe. This connection could be a coincidence, but it's far more likely that when McCartney was writing this song, he chose the blackbird specifically to represent a group of people who needed to hear a song of hope and support during a difficult time.

It wasn't until well after the song's release that McCartney began to discuss "Blackbird" and its connection to racial strife in America. According to

Steve Turner, "nowadays, when performing it in concert, [McCartney] claims that it was written 'when there were troubles in the southern states of America over civil rights and I was hoping that by writing this song I might bring a little hope to the people going through the struggles'" (McCartney, quoted in Turner, 2015, p. 245). The song is featured on nearly every, if not every, concert setlist McCartney plays. Now, this brings us to another facet of Blackbird's creation story, because it ties into a McCartney concert.

According to a 2016 article by Daniel Kreps, and corroborated by McCartney himself on Twitter, Blackbird has another origin story: the story of the Little Rock Nine. Now, for any readers that don't know the story of the Little Rock Nine, we will take a moment to review the history. "In 1954 the United States Supreme Court ruled that segregated schools were illegal. The case, Brown v. The Board of Education, has become iconic for Americans because it marked the formal beginning of the end of segregation" (National Museum of African American History & Culture, n.d.). The legislation, however, didn't mean that segregation within schools wasn't going to happen: unfortunately, it took time for people to accept what the Supreme Court's ruling would mean to their everyday lives. That said, in 1957 the Little Rock Nine:

> "as the nine teens came to be known, were to be the first African American students to enter Little Rock's Central High School. Three years earlier, following the Supreme Court ruling, the Little Rock school board pledged to voluntarily desegregate its schools. This idea was explosive for the community and, like much of the South, it was fraught with anger and bitterness" (National Museum of African American History & Culture, n.d.).

Now, the Little Rock Nine didn't have an easy time getting into the school: they were blocked by mobs, police, and the National Guard. In the end, it took until September 25, 1957 for the Little Rock Nine to be able to attend classes consistently. Now, this was occurring much before the writing of the song "Blackbird," but according to McCartney, it was a part of the inspiration for the song. In 2016, while McCartney was on tour, he was able to meet two members of the Little Rock Nine - Thelma Mothershed Wair and Elizabeth Eckford - at one of his concerts. He introduced the song at the concert thusly:

> Way back in the Sixties, there was a lot of trouble going on over civil rights, particularly in Little Rock. We would notice this on the news back in England, so it's a really important place for us, because to me, this is where civil rights started. We would see what was going on and sympathize with the people going through those troubles, and it made me want to write a song that, if it ever got back to the people going through those troubles, it might just help them a little bit, and that's this next one (McCartney, quoted in Kreps, 2016).

McCartney also posted to Twitter to confirm his stance that the Little Rock Nine played a part in inspiring the story of "Blackbird," saying that it was "incredible to meet two of the Little Rock Nine - pioneers of the civil rights movement and inspiration for Blackbird" (McCartney, quoted in Kreps, 2016).

As we'll learn in a future section, when we discuss the infamous "Helter Skelter," many of the songs on the Beatles White Album were taken out of context by serial killer Charles Manson. Charles Manson believed that the Beatles were prophets, warning him of the impending racial Armageddon, and informing him of what actions he should take. According to Manson, "'Blackbird' was an invitation for the black people of the world to destroy the white man" (Blake, 2004). Manson "figured the Beatles were programming the black people to get it up, get it on, start doing it," with lyrics like "Blackbird singing in the dead of night/ Take these broken wings and learn to fly ... You were only waiting for this moment to arise. Rise' was one of Charlie's big words" (Jakobson, quoted in Grow, 2019). The phrase 'rise' impacted Manson specifically, because he painted it in blood on the wall after one of his murders. Though this doesn't relate at all to the intent of the song, it is important to note that the song was grossly misinterpreted in one case, and for a while became associated with Charles Manson, something the Beatles never planned nor intended.

Now that we've had an opportunity to explore the various stories behind "Blackbird," let's take a moment to consider the song in musical terms: what is it about the musical aspects of "Blackbird" that make it so appealing to such a wide audience? Let's take a look in the studio when "Blackbird" was recorded. The song was a solo recording by Paul McCartney, who was playing a Martin D 28 acoustic guitar. You'll remember, dear reader, that we discussed different types of guitars in the introduction to this book, and learned that acoustic guitars don't require amplification and provide a certain mood to songs. This song is likely one of the best examples of the perfect use of an acoustic guitar, as the song is only made up of four aspects: vocals, guitar, tapping, and the blackbird sound. Now, the tapping sound was originally attributed to a metronome, but that is, in fact, incorrect: the tapping is actually a specific recording of McCartney tapping his feet as he plays the song. The sound of the blackbird was edited in after the original recording sessions.

"Blackbird" is played in the key of G major, which according to the University of Michigan, represents "everything rustic, idyllic and lyrical, every calm and satisfied passion, every tender gratitude for true friendship and faithful love,--in a word every gentle and peaceful emotion of the heart is correctly expressed by this key" (University of Michigan, n.d.). Though the topic of the song is everything but gentle and peaceful, the intent of the song is exactly that: to provide a calm and peaceful hope to those who needed it. As always, the Beatles put the song in the key that made most sense, both musically and meaningfully.

McCartney "often cites 'Blackbird' as evidence that the best of his songs come spontaneously, when words and music tumble out as if they had already been formulated without conscious effort on his behalf" (Turner, 2015, p. 245). That said, it's likely that McCartney subconsciously put in a fair amount of effort to imbue this song with meaning; after all, it is one of his most recognized, most famous, and most covered songs. "Blackbird" is hauntingly beautiful, and carries with it a message of hope, specifically intended to those who are fighting for their rights, but also for anyone who needs to believe that they can rise and once again learn to fly.

The Ballad of John and Yoko

Standing in the dock at Southampton

Trying to get to Holland or France

The man in the mac said

"You've got to go back"

You know, they didn't even give us a chance

Christ, you know it ain't easy

You know how hard it can be

The way things are going

They're going to crucify me

Finally made the plane into Paris

Honeymooning down by the Seine

Peter Brown called to say

You can make it okay

You can get married in Gibraltar near Spain

Christ, you know it ain't easy

You know how hard it can be

The way things are going

They're going to crucify me

Drove from Paris to the Amsterdam Hilton

Talking in our beds for a week

The news people said

"Say, what you doing in bed?"

I said, "We're only trying to get us some peace"

Christ, you know it ain't easy

You know how hard it can be

The way things are going

They're going to crucify me

Saving up your money for a rainy day

Giving all your clothes to charity

Last night the wife said

Oh boy, when you're dead

You don't take nothing with you but your soul

Think!

Made a lightning trip to Vienna

Eating chocolate cake in a bag

Newspapers said

"She's gone to his head

They look just like two gurus in drag"

Christ, you know it ain't easy

You know how hard it can be

The way things are going

They're going to crucify me

Caught the early plane back to London

Fifty acorns tied in a sack

The men from the press

Said, "We wish you success

It's good to have the both of you back"

Christ, you know it ain't easy

You know how hard it can be

The way things are going

They're going to crucify me

The way things are going

They're going to crucify me

"The Ballad of John and Yoko" is a song that is quite controversial amongst fans. For some fans it is a testament of John and Yoko's strength as a couple to withstand hardships and strive for peace, some find it be about more useless peace and love talk without any action being spewed by rich celebrities, and some just find it be a adventurous tune with a fun and bouncy musical backing. One thing is for certain: the track left an impression on fans. Functioning as the B-side to the single "Get Back," the song was never released on an official Beatles LP, which makes sense when looking back at the reaction the song has received. The product of an especially inspired recording session over one night from Lennon and McCartney, holds a bluesy sway while also keeping a fairly adventurous and upbeat tempo, pairing well with the adventures that John and Yoko embark on in the song (Pollack, 1999).

From a storytelling perspective, it wasn't odd for the Beatles to incorporate autobiographical elements into their songs. Where "The Ballad of John and Yoko" differs though is that it is entirely a non-fictional story -- at least from John Lennon's perspective. The song, absolutely one of the more divisive songs in the Beatles extensive catalogue, details the trials and tribulations that John and Yoko had to endure in their pursuit of marriage, as well as their infamous honeymoon that followed which itself was an incredibly controversial high-profile event. By this point in their career, everyone around the world was interested in what the Beatles were doing. John and Yoko, understanding of this, decided to use that interest to their advantage. For their honeymoon, which began on March 20th in the Presidential Suite at the Hilton in Amsterdam, they invited the press into their bedroom daily from 10:00 am to 10:00 pm where they would be staying in bed for peace. The purpose from John and Yoko's perspective was to entice the press' hunger for headlining Beatles news, but to ultimately be met with answers regarding the dream of world peace from the two famous lovers dressed in pajamas (Turner, 2015).

John, not one to shy away from controversy, incites some on this track as well with lyrics like "The way things are going, they're gonna crucify me." In fact the song was controversial enough that radio stations edited out the word Christ (Stark, 261, 2005). However, this is not the only time that Lennon compared himself or the Beatles to Jesus Christ either. In 1966 he famously asserted that the Beatles were bigger than Jesus Christ with how many people were infatuated with them. The quote from the London Evening Standard article written by Maureen Cleave reads:

> "Christianity will go," he said. "It will vanish and shrink. I needn't argue about that; I'm right and I will be proved right. We're more popular than Jesus now; I don't know which will go first -- rock 'n' roll or Christianity. Jesus was all right but his disciples were thick and ordinary. It's them twisting it that ruins it for me" (1966).

These comments in turn caused mass backlash against the group, most famously in the American Bible Belt where their music was banned on many radio stations and public burnings of their records were prevalent (Sullivan, 1987). While this backlash against this track may not have been as severe as they were against his comments three years earlier, they do help show off Lennon's personality and the face he showed to the public. That face, of course, is one that was unafraid of other's reaction to him, which helped ensure that Lennon would whatever he could to communicate his ideas to the world at large.

In Lennon's attempt to describe his struggles with his at times overwhelming celebrity life, he uses metaphors relating himself to Jesus Christ in hopes of describing what he feels is the burden of celebrity life. In focusing on this aspect of "The Ballad of John and Yoko" as well as Lennon's past controversial statements on the subject, Nathan Timmons states in his paper *John, Paul, Jorge, and Ringo: Borges, Beatles, and the Metaphor of Celebrity Crucifixion*:

> "Lennon thus interprets his experiences as a famous musician through the lens of sacred story; just as Christ's overwhelming popularity eventually contributed to his crucifixion, a death called for by the same crowds who had earlier worshiped him, 'The Ballad of John and Yoko' suggests that the songwriter, in

light of what had taken place for him and the Beatles since 1966, nervously anticipated a metaphoric repetition of biblical events in his own life. Such are the consequences, Lennon might have reasoned, for those who assume the mantle of venerated and mythologized cultural leader. Given his tumultuous relationship with fame, though, one must question whether Lennon perceived his public crucifixion at this time as something to be avoided or instead precipitated" (2011).

The details of the story that Lennon omitted while writing a song where he is portraying himself as near equal to Jesus Christ, a man who lived without sin, seemed to just be asking for more controversy from the Chrisitan audience just as he had done three years prior. In the chorus of the song Lennon appears to be talking with Jesus not quite as an equal but as someone who each could relate to one another. The line "They're gonna crucify me" adds to this idea of Lennon speaking to someone who is able to relate to his woes. The "they're" Lennon speaks of in the song can be interpreted as the public. That is the fans, the press, and all of those in-between. Lennon had reached such a level of superstardom at this point in his career that anything he would do or say would be pushed into the public sphere for all to discuss, debate, and discredit.

While there is something to be said of John's struggle in differentiating his personal life and public face, as well as his relationship with the world at large as a celebrity, there are parts of this song where Lennon does take liberties in his complaints. The line "Standing in the dock at Southampton/ trying to get to Holland or France/ the man in the mac said 'you've got to go back'/ you know, they didn't even give us a chance" may suggest to the listener that John and Yoko were turned away because of a reason out of their control. On the contrary, the reason they were turned away was because the couple did not have passports when trying to fly to France (Turner, 2015). Another point of question comes where Lennon asserts that they "finally made the plane into Paris." Based on this line it may be understood that Lennon and Ono were finally able to board a passenger plane, though in reality they had found their way onto a private executive plane in order to get there.

This song is also contentious within Beatles fandom due to its subject and the dislike some have for Yoko. Dating back to when the Beatles broke up, there have been those who believe that it was Yoko who broke up the Beatles due to her influence on John. This seems to come from an interview with Lennon conducted by Jann S. Wenner and published in the issue of Rolling Stone dated January 21st, 1971 in which he stated: "I had to either be married to them or Yoko, and I chose Yoko, and I was right" (1971).

This, as well as reports that the other Beatles despised her, caused Yoko to become the figurehead in the group's break-up. However, while Yoko was not well liked by the group it would be untrue and particularly cruel to place the blame onto her. The Beatles, as noted by John, Paul, George and Ringo, had been drifting apart since the death of Brian Epstein. The Beatles were four talented people who over time, as is the case with human beings, changed and grew in different directions than one another. Ono herself has said as much stating that "I think that each of the Beatles was too strong and tough an individual to have been influenced by me in any way" (Cott, 89, 2013). So the assertion that Yoko is the one who caused the breakup is misguided, usually evolving out of emotions that are at best based out of coping with the end of something loved and at worst based upon sexist and racist ideas. In the end, the decision was each member of the Beatles and theirs alone.

"The Ballad of John and Yoko" is a Beatles track that remains controversial to this day. As a story, some fans are quick to point out Lennon's role as an unreliable narrator to his own story, lightly twisting facts from reality to the lyrics sheet. This is a valid criticism of the song, but it muddies the idea that this song speaks to Lennon's truth: a truth not entirely based within fact or typical reason, but based upon John's emotions during this tumultuous time in his and Yoko's lives. Storytelling doesn't always have to provide a reader with absolute facts, but a good story should convey emotional truths to it's listener, allowing them to not only visualize the story but to feel the emotions within the text. It is in this aspect of storytelling that "The Ballad of John and Yoko" ultimately succeeds.

The Continuing Story of Bungalow Bill

Hey, Bungalow Bill

What did you kill

Bungalow Bill?

Hey, Bungalow Bill

What did you kill

Bungalow Bill?

He went out tiger hunting with his elephant and gun

In case of accidents he always took his mum

He's the all American bullet-headed saxon mother's son

All the children sing

Hey, Bungalow Bill

What did you kill

Bungalow Bill?

Hey, Bungalow Bill

What did you kill

Bungalow Bill?

Deep in the jungle where the mighty tiger lies

The BEATLES

Bill and his elephants were taken by surprise

So Captain Marvel zapped him right between the eyes

All the children sing

Hey, Bungalow Bill

What did you kill

Bungalow Bill?

Hey, Bungalow Bill

What did you kill

Bungalow Bill?

The children asked him if to kill was not a sin

"Not when he looked so fierce", his mummy butted in

"If looks could kill it would have been us instead of him"

All the children sing

Hey, Bungalow Bill

What did you kill

Bungalow Bill?

Hey, Bungalow Bill

What did you kill

Bungalow Bill?

Hey, Bungalow Bill

What did you kill

Bungalow Bill?

Hey, Bungalow Bill

What did you kill

Bungalow Bill?

Hey, Bungalow Bill

What did you kill

Bungalow Bill?

Hey, Bungalow Bill

What did you kill

Bungalow Bill?

Hey, Bungalow Bill

What did you kill

Bungalow Bill?

Hey, Bungalow Bill

What did you kill

Bungalow Bill?

The late period Beatles are known for their imaginative lyrics that help the listener visualize the environment and characters of the song, while the early Beatle songs are often very relatable for the viewer, speaking of subjects of common desire or indignation. In "The Continuing Tale of Bungalow Bill" the group sort of combines the imaginative and playful lyrics that they produce in the time period that this song was written, with the direct and clear lyrics that tell a story easy to understand.

"The Continuing Story of Bungalow Bill" is another track off of the Beatles eponymous project that focuses on harkening to the music that they loved while telling compelling stories through fun and at times sarcastically cutting lyrics. This song was also written in India around the same time that "Rocky Raccoon" was being written by Paul. Interestingly enough, both tracks owe something to and take reference from American popular culture. Rocky Raccoon takes influence from the gunslinging western genre that was a popular export from America. "Bungalow Bill" also pulls from American pop culture, in which references are used primarily to describe it's all-american protagonist.

"Bungalow Bill" was written primarily by John in reference to an American man the group had met during their time in India. Richard Cooke III and his mother went on a hunting excursion while there, much to the dismay of Maharishi Mahesh Yogi and seemingly to John as well. In Steve Turner's book *A Hard Day's Write*, Cooke explains that Cooke got along well with most of the Beatles, except for John. Lennon, very much focused on counterculture and criticism of the institutions that had long held a grip on certain aspects of society, didn't seem to see much in Cooke (Cooke, quoted in Turner, 2005, p. 155).

"[...] He went out tiger hunting with his elephant and gun

In case of accidents he always took his mum

He's the all American bullet-headed saxon mother's son [...]"

Lennon's distaste for the young American comes through loud and clear in the first verse. Here Lennon plays up the role of the hunter in the first line, out to find a tiger with two powerful allies by his side. The idea of the strong hunter comes tumbling down in the second line where the narrator insists that the big, strong hunter still needs to take his mother with him "in case of accidents." This is only followed by the narrator describing him as a typical American momma's boy. By this point the listener understands that the narrator thinks of the protagonist as pathetic at best.

"[...] Deep in the jungle where the mighty tiger lies

Bill and his elephants were taken by surprise

So Captain Marvel zapped him right between the eyes [...]"

The second verse focuses on the hunt itself, where Richard and his mother were supposedly taken by surprise as the tiger seemingly found them first. This verse also continues to poke fun at Bungalow Bill. By calling him Captain Marvel the narrator furthers the idea that not only is he the prototypical patriotic American man, but also pokes fun at him either for seeing himself as a superhero for killing the tiger or is more critically pointing out the power dynamic between the man and the animal. Either way, the narrator continues to mock the titular character of the song, which can be seen as Lennon mocking Cooke.

"[...] The children asked him if to kill was not a sin

'Not when he looked so fierce', his mummy butted in

'If looks could kill it would have been us instead of him [...]'"

The last verse of the song details the aftermath of Bill's tiger hunt. As children interrogate him, asking if his actions were a sin. Bill and his mother take an immediate defensive position, blaming the tiger for its own death due to the fear it caused them when they ultimately made the active decision to go on a hunt for a tiger. This verse also mirrors the reality of Cooke and his mother's violent deed. When the two returned to the retreat they attempted to keep the hunt a secret. Well, Richard did at least.

It wasn't long before Richards' mother was keen to tell others about their exploits. Upon hearing of the news some were not impressed, notably the Beatles and Maharishi himself. It was during the two's conversation with Maharishi with John and Paul sitting nearby where John asked "Don't you call that slightly life-destructive" with Cooke responding "it was either the tiger or us. The tiger was jumping right where we were" (Cooke, quoted in Turner, 2005, p. 155). This interaction seems to have been pulled by John directly into the song, and specifically this last verse.

Finally, in the chorus of the song the children ask Bungalow Bill what he killed. These lines go together with the first line of the third verse where the children ask him if killing is a sin, almost in a manner to reassure themselves that it indeed is. The children being so pushy with Bill also shows how much he was hoping to hide from others, not willing to let his actions spill out. Whether this was because he felt ashamed for his actions, or that he just didn't want to feel shamed by others we will never know.

While the song is based on the real life events of Richard Cooke III, there are references within the song to popular culture figures within. Notably is the namesake that Lennon gives to Richard, "Bungalow Bill." While Bill is used in the song to refer to Richard, Bungalow Bill is most likely an allusion to Buffalo Bill (Turner, 2005, p. 155). William Frederick Cody, better known as Buffalo Bill, was a real larger than life figure of his own. One of the most well known cowboys of his time, William Frederick Cody was a man to take notice of. At a time one of the most sought after scouts and huntsmen in America, Cody would take all of his knowledge of the west to his travelling show that would make him a global star. Being one of the first huge stars from America, it only makes sense that Lennon would allude to him when writing about Cooke. However, this begs the question why did Lennon replace Buffalo with Bungalow? It seems that the inclusion of Bungalow into the protagonist's name is due to the fact that residents of Maharishi's spiritual retreat often stayed in bungalows on the property (Turner, 2005, p. 155).

In terms of the recording of the song, there is an element used to further incorporate the listener's engagement with the story being told. That element is Yoko Ono. Ono was chosen to play the role of the mother in the song (Stark, 2005, 237). Yoko makes an appearance on the track as she sings the line "[...]Not when he looked so fierce." The line, being spoken by the mother character in the track, is that of a mother trying to protect her son from ridicule; no matter how warranted that ridicule may be. This appearance has become a landmark moment in the Beatles recording history, as Yoko's appearance is the first and last time a woman would sing a lead vocal part in a Beatles song.

"The Continuing Story of Bungalow Bill," another song penned by Lennon, shows off his willingness to create a narrative based on events that have taken place in his own life. In this track the listener is given Lennon's emotional truth of the situation, but also a taste of his sarcastic humour as he continuously pokes fun at the American. It is also another track off of *The Beatles* that displays the group's creativity and willingness to play with genre, medium, and cultural influences as to not be pigeon-holed into one specific type of socially accepted musical storytelling.

Maxwell's Silver Hammer

Joan was quizzical

Studied pataphysical science in the home

Late nights all alone with a test tube

Oh, oh, oh, oh

Maxwell Edison, majoring in medicine

Calls her on the phone

"Can I take you out to the pictures, Joa-o-o-oan?"

But as she's getting ready to go

A knock comes on the door

Bang! Bang! Maxwell's silver hammer

Came down upon her head

Clang! Clang! Maxwell's silver hammer

Made sure that she was dead

Back in school again, Maxwell plays the fool again

Teacher gets annoyed

Wishing to avoid an unpleasant scene

She tells Max to stay when the class has gone away

So he waits behind

Writing fifty times "I must not be so"

But when she turns her back on the boy

He creeps up from behind

Bang! Bang! Maxwell's silver hammer

Came down upon her head

Clang! Clang! Maxwell's silver hammer

Made sure that she was dead

P. C. Thirty-One

Said "We caught a dirty one"

Maxwell stands alone

Painting testimonial pictures

Oh, oh, oh, oh

Rose and Valerie, screaming from the gallery

Say he must go free (Maxwell must go free)

The judge does not agree, and he tells them so

But as the words are leaving his lips

A noise comes from behind

Bang! Bang! Maxwell's silver hammer

Came down upon his head

Clang! Clang! Maxwell's silver hammer

Made sure that he was dead

Wo-wo-wo-woh

Silver hammer man

No book about Beatles storytelling songs would be complete without the worthy inclusion of "Maxwell's Silver Hammer." Between the philosophy that inspired the song, the way three quarters of the Beatles absolutely despised the song, the way the story is told within the song, and the curious practice of taking on topics of death and destruction with a positive feel for the song, there are a ton of ideas to unpack here. Our discussion of this song will take us to a variety of interesting places, and will leave us feeling enlightened and more knowledgeable about the events and stories that led to the creation of "Maxwell's Silver Hammer."

Let's begin our analysis of "Maxwell's Silver Hammer" by discussing the philosophical theory that both inspired the song and the first character in the song: 'pataphysics. 'Pataphysics is a particularly curious form of science that actually has more than 100 definitions - all of them correct. Before we dive into the discussion of 'pataphysics, it's important to note that the actual concept of 'pataphysics is fairly difficult to grasp, but the authors aspire to provide the most detailed explanation possible while still adhering to the guidelines of 'pataphysics.

The first definition of 'pataphysics that we will entertain is this:

> 'Pataphysics is the science of that which is superinduced upon metaphysics, whether within or beyond the latter's limitations, extending as far beyond metaphysics as the latter extends beyond physics. ... 'Pataphysics will be, above all, the science of the particular, despite the common opinion that the only science is that of the general. 'Pataphysics will examine the laws governing exceptions, and will explain the universe supplementary to this one (Jarry, 1996, p. 21).

Now, this definition of 'pataphysics may seem particularly confusing; in fact, that's its functional intention. At its essence, 'pataphysics is a joke intended to be a parody of science itself: a concept that, if taken too seriously, ruins the joke itself. That said, 'pataphysics has also held and continues to hold a particular amount of influence within literature, music, and in visual arts. As Marcus O'Dair notes: Though 'pataphysics can be seen as a philosophical prank, it's hard to knock a concept widely acknowledged to have paved the way for Dada, Futurism, Surrealism, and the Theatre of the Absurd" (2014). Even though 'pataphysics was intended as a joke, it became something much more than that, which appears to add onto the joke itself. To better understand the reach of 'pataphysics, and some of the concepts that have come from it, let's take a deeper dive into this curiously confusing theory.

First, let's explore the grammatical elephant in the room. If you've been reading along and wondering why we authors are always including an apostrophe in front of 'pataphysics, you're not alone. It isn't a mistake from the author or editor however; it's actually a required part of the title itself. The creator of 'pataphysics, Alfred Jarry, was French, and most of the creation of 'pataphysics was actually completed in French. The Museum of Patamechanics (which may or may not actually exist), explains the presence and absence of the apostrophe thusly:

> Jarry mandated the inclusion of the apostrophe in the orthography, 'pataphysique and 'pataphysics, "to avoid a simple pun" – however, the pun intended is left unclear. The words pataphysician or pataphysicist and the adjective pataphysical usually do not (and some command should not) include the apostrophe. This mater [sic] was ruled upon by his late Magnificence, the Vice-Curator-Founder of the Collège de 'Pataphysique in which he stipulates that only when consciously referring to Jarry's use of the word or his Science should the word 'pataphysics carry the apostrophe. Hence its omission in some palaces on the website and the inclusion in others (2021).

Just like the definition of 'pataphysics itself, the rules behind when to and when not to place an apostrophe in front of 'pataphysics are purposefully unclear. This example, and the example provided by the Museum of Patamechanics' website - which both confirms and denies the existence of a physical museum - demonstrates the true intent of 'pataphysics. In the same way, the College of 'Pataphysics both confirms and denies its existence on its website, and claims "to study these most important and serious of all problems : the only ones that are important and serious" (2021). Logically, the motto of the school is *Eadem mutata resurgo*: I arise again the same though changed.

Now, readers, this discussion of 'pataphysics was important and provided to you for a reason more than just scrambling your brains with the confusion of 'pataphysics. The fact is that 'pataphysics played a particularly prominent role in "Maxwell's Silver Hammer," because it was after hearing a recording of a play by 'pataphysics creator Alfred Jarry in 1966 that McCartney became fascinated with the idea of 'pataphysics. About the play, McCartney said: "it was the best radio play I had ever heard in my life, and the best production, and Ubu was so brilliantly played. It was just a sensation. That was one of the big things of the period for me" (McCartney, quoted in Beatles Bible, 2021). McCartney then took in a version of the play live later in the year, and became extremely interested in the concept of 'pataphysics.

Barry Miles, a close friend of McCartney's, was also interested in 'pataphysics - so much so that "he had been made a member of the College of Pataphysics and awarded the Ordre de la Grande Gidouille for pataphysical activity" (Beatles Bible, 2021). Since no one else in McCartney's life had taken to 'pataphysics the same way that he and Barry had, it was a pleasant chance for him to connect to the topic with a friend. It was from these conversations, and the fact that very few people actually knew about 'pataphysics, that the inclusion of 'pataphysics in "Maxwell's Silver Hammer" was born. About this, McCartney says:

> Miles and I often used to talk about the pataphysical society and the Chair of Applied Alcoholism. So I put that in one of the Beatles songs, 'Maxwell's Silver Hammer': "Joan was quizzical, studied pataphysical science in the home…" Nobody knows what it means; I only explained it to Linda just the other day. That's the lovely thing about it. I am the only person who ever put the name

of pataphysics into the record charts, c'mon! It was great. I love those surreal little touches (McCartney, quoted in Miles, 1997).

Readers, our new understanding - or lack thereof - of 'pataphysics is helpful in more than just understanding its brief reference within the song; in fact, it helps us better understand the song overall. Though the song follows a story pattern, there are parts of the story that are simply unexplainable, and that's where 'pataphysics comes in. Let's outline the story within "Maxwell's Silver Hammer." First, Maxwell calls Joan, a 'pataphysics student, and invites her to see a movie. Then, Maxwell knocks on her door and kills her with his silver hammer. After that, Maxwell is found in his classroom (it's noted that he's a medicine student) and is called out for acting out. Once he is given lines to write as punishment for his misbehaviour, he waits for the teacher to turn her back and then kills her with his silver hammer. Finally, Maxwell is caught by the police, and during his trial, Maxwell kills the judge in the same way he did Joan and his teacher: with a knock on the head from his silver hammer.

Now, as stories go, there are a fair amount of questions and plot holes existing in this one. First, why would Maxwell bother calling Joan and inviting her to a movie if he was simply going to kill her anyway? How would he get away with it long enough to end up back in his medicine classes? In addition, what university professor would give out lines to a student? That action has a bit of an elementary school feel to it - not something that would typically occur in a higher education class. Finally, there's the question of how on earth Maxwell goes from being on trial for his crimes after being arrested (and likely his hammer being confiscated as evidence) to sneaking up behind the judge and killing him in a courtroom with said hammer. Now, we authors recognize that a part of 'pataphysics is not exploring a concept or the concept so intensely that it ruins the joke, and we also know that an easy answer to all of the above questions is: it's a song, so it doesn't have to make sense, and the plot is made up based on the best ways in which the story came together lyrically. It's arguable, however, that based on McCartney's previous writing credits and his newfound affection for 'pataphysics, that these plot holes aren't actually holes at all, but are in fact purposeful.

Now, in order to explore why these plot holes, or unanswerable questions, might be purposeful, let's take a quick dive into some of the previous stories that McCartney has written within his songs. He wrote "Paperback Writer," which as we saw in a previous section, is about much more than just a writer wanting to sell its book; it tells the story of the paperback revolution, stemming back decades from when McCartney wrote the song. He wrote "The Fool on the Hill" which was about more than just a fool: it centered around a misunderstood visionary. We could go on all day listing the many incredible writing credits that McCartney had by this time in his Beatles career and still not cover all of the amazing songs and amazing, in-depth stories that they tell. In all of those songs, the story circle is complete: there's never any questions left at the end of the song that aren't intended to be left there. It raises a red flag, then, that there are so many unanswered questions at the end of "Maxwell's Silver Hammer," simply because it's out of character for McCartney.

We know, of course, that this song was purely and quintessentially McCartney: in fact, John Lennon hated the song and didn't attend recording sessions - in part due to his need to recover from a recent automobile accident - and his only credit to the song is in the songwriting Lennon-McCartney duo. George Harrison was reasonably indifferent to the song, though he was irritated by the amount of time it took to record. Ringo Starr, on the other hand, felt very strongly about the song, saying that "The worst session ever was 'Maxwell's Silver Hammer'. It was the worst track we ever had to record. It went on for fucking weeks. I thought it was mad" (Starr, quoted in Beatles Bible, 2021). With these ringing endorsements for the song, it's not hard to understand that none of the other Beatles wanted anything to do with its recording, let alone its writing. So, we are left with the knowledge that these lyrics and the song itself are pure McCartney.

We will be discussing the recording of the song later on in this section, but now, we will be moving on to the ways in which, based on 'pataphysics, "Maxwell's Silver Hammer" actually does make sense. The key fact about 'pataphysics that we have to remember, is that it is the science of imaginary solutions. Based on that logic, there's no end to what can be true under 'pataphysical law. In that way, then, all the questions that listeners are left with at the end of "Maxwell's Siver Hammer" are meaningless because we can imagine solutions that are invariably true. If we wanted to imagine that to kill the judge, Maxwell grew wings and summoned his hammer like Thor, by the laws of 'pataphysics, our imaginary solution would be correct. In the same way, if we thought that Maxwell's identical twin was actually the one arrested, and the real Maxwell was hiding in the courtroom waiting for his moment, 'pataphysics says that we would also be correct. It's not difficult to imagine McCartney appreciating this logic, and leaving these questions purposefully for listeners to engage with, so that whatever solution they came up with, according to the logic of the theory the song was built upon, the listeners would always be right.

That said, McCartneys did have a reason for writing the song that was more grounded in reality. As he explains to Barry Miles:

> 'Maxwell's Silver Hammer' was my analogy for when something goes wrong out of the blue, as it so often does, as I was beginning to find out at that time in my life. I wanted something symbolic of that, so to me it was some fictitious character called Maxwell with a silver hammer. I don't know why it was silver, it just sounded better than Maxwell's hammer. It was needed for scanning. We still use that expression even now when something unexpected happens (McCartney, quoted in Miles, 1997).

As we all know, unexpected things can hit us like a ton of bricks and come from out of nowhere: we constantly have to be on our toes and ready for whatever comes next. McCartney wanted "Maxwell's Silver Hammer" to reflect this state of nature. Of course, this is a more morbid reflection of this nature than most, but McCartney did have a tendency of taking some really heavy topics and dressing them up using different musical tendencies.

One of his post-Beatles hits "My Brave Face" really demonstrates this tendency, as it discusses the loss of his wife to cancer, but is still an upbeat and happy-sounding song, contrasting directly with the lyrics themselves.

That said, it's important for us to explore the lyrics of this song in comparison to the musical aspects of the song, just like we did earlier for "Misery." You'll remember that in that section, we explored Jacob Jolji's Feel Good Index for songs, which rates songs on their feel-good energy using three categories: a song's lyrics, its tempo in beats per minute, and its key. Let;s take a moment and explore these categories in relation to "Maxwell's Silver Hammer," so we can reconcile the reason its lyrics sound so dark and dreary (it is, after all, a song about a serial killer), but it sounds and feels like a more happy and energetic song.

Of course, then, for the first category, lyrics, the song would rate on the low end of the feel good scale, as it's about a serial killer who kills people by hitting them on the head with a hammer. The lyrics are catchy though, and are the type that would get stuck in your head or be easy to hum unthinkingly, but that doesn't make their subject matter any less serious and upsetting. "Maxwell's Silver Hammer" is played at 129 beats per minute, which gives it fairly high energy and, according to the Get Song BPM website, high danceability points as well (2021). The ideal beats per minute for jogging is between 120 and 130 bpm, so this song could, theoretically, be categorized as a good workout song. In the beats per minute category of the Feel Good Index, then, "Maxwell's Silver Hammer" scores fairly high. Finally, "Maxwell's Silver Hammer" is played in the key D Major, which according to the University of Michigan is "The key of triumph, of Hallejuahs [sic], of war-cries, of victory-rejoicing. Thus, the inviting symphonies, the marches, holiday songs and heaven-rejoicing choruses are set in this key" (n.d.). The song feels triumphant and exciting, which is yet another reason that though its lyrics are sinister, its musical elements feel energized and victorious.

This quick analysis using the Feel Good Index is particularly helpful when it comes to helping us understand why songs make us feel certain ways. We would expect that since "Maxwell's Silver Hammer" is about a serial killer, that it wouldn't make us feel as energized as it does, but thanks to the Feel Good Index, we can understand what aspects of the song make us feel certain ways, and why. Of course, it was McCartney's intention to make the song and the lyrics clash in terms of energy, but it was something he did oh so well. That leads us into the next part of our conversation about "Maxwell's Silver Hammer:" its recording and release intent.

When Paul McCartney wrote "Maxwell's Silver Hammer," he imagined it as the Beatles' next single. Because of that belief, and in spite of none of the other Beatles actually liking the song, he put extra work into the song in the studio to ensure it was going to be perfect. The original recording date was January 3, 1969, and subsequent recording dates included January 7, 8, and 10, of the same year. Because the other Beatles didn't particularly like the song, they felt as if the recording sessions were dragging on and on, though the actual recording of the song lasted at much less time than the 'weeks' that Ringo Starr said it took. John Lennon noted that McCartney "did everything to make it into a single and it never was and it never could've been," (Lennon, quoted in Beatles Bible, 2021). In the end, Lennon was right: despite McCartney's efforts to make "Maxwell's Silver Hammer" a single, it was released on the *Abbey Road* album in the fall of 1969, and never did become a Beatles single.

"Maxwell's Silver Hammer" is a curious Beatles song for many reasons: its subject matter, history, and the way in which it's written. That said, now that we've had the chance to explore these aspects, it's as if the song has become even more curious in all the right ways. From its roots in the confusing 'pataphysics to the reactions from other Beatles members, "Maxwell's Silver Hammer" is a McCartney story song for the record books, and will remain a memorable and catchy tune in the minds and ears of everyone who hears it.

Section 3: Honourable Mentions

Introduction

There are stories attached to hundreds of Beatles songs, and books upon books have been filled with those stories. Of course, it's simply impossible to fully explore all stories the Beatles included in their songs in this specific book, so the stories we explored in the previous section were painstakingly selected to ensure an optimum mix of stories within songs, stories about songs, and analysis of the ways these stories existed within these songs. With that in mind, we have to consider the fact that there are a few Beatles songs that have fascinating stories surrounding them that don't quite fit the categories within which the songs in the previous section were selected. That said, it's only natural to want to further dive into some fascinating Beatles history and legacies within additional songs; after all, there's no shortage of intriguing stories in Beatles songs.

The following three songs were selected for various reasons, but predominantly because of the fascinating stories attached to them: not stories the Beatles necessarily intended to tell, but stories that have become fundamentally and intrinsically woven into the basis of these songs. From satirizing the "Paul is Dead" conspiracy theory to analyzing the true meaning of the Beatles' move to becoming a studio band, "Sgt. Pepper's Lonely Hearts Club Band," "Glass Onion," and "Helter Skelter" are three truly fascinating Beatles songs with some unbelievably interesting stories behind them. Now, it's time for us to move forward from the stories the Beatles intended to tell, and explore some more unintentional, yet successful, storytelling opportunities.

Sgt. Pepper's Lonely Hearts Club Band

It was 20 years ago today

Sgt. Pepper taught the band to play

They've been going in and out of style

But they're guaranteed to raise a smile

So may I introduce to you

The act you've know for all these years

Sgt. Pepper's Lonely Hearts Club Band

We're Sgt. Pepper's Lonely Hearts Club Band

We hope you will enjoy the show

Sgt. Pepper's Lonely Hearts Club Band

Sit back and let the evening go

Sgt. Pepper's Lonely, Sgt. Pepper's Lonely

Sgt. Pepper's Lonely Hearts Club Band

It's wonderful to be here

It's certainly a thrill

You're such a lovely audience

We'd like to take you home with us

We'd love to take you home

I don't really want to stop the show

But I thought that you might like to know

That the singer's gonna sing a song

And he wants you all to sing along

So let me introduce to you

The one and only Billy Shears

And Sgt. Pepper's Lonely Hearts Club Band, yeah

'Sgt. Pepper's Lonely Hearts Club Band' represents so much more than just the above lyrics, which is why it is truly fascinating to explore, and moreover, why it absolutely deserves a spot in our honourable mentions category. From the shift it represented in the Beatles' public appearances to the freedom Sgt. Pepper provided them as a band, the song itself is a gateway into a particularly interesting and engaging story about a band wanting to transcend global expectations and take a stab at creating something new; which for a globally renowned band was quite a feat.

To begin our exploration, let's discuss what the album *Sgt. Pepper's Lonely Hearts Club Band* represented for the Beatles. Of course, the only place to begin in a discussion like this is with some historical context: if we can insert ourselves in certain moments in history to provide ourselves with the understanding of the time, we will be better placed to comprehend the overall story of how Sgt. Pepper came to be. Our story begins, then, in the summer of 1966, as the high that the Beatles had been riding throughout Beatlemania finally began to drop.

June of 1966 welcomed a new Beatles compilation album to the world: *Yesterday and Today*. Now, the contents of the album weren't the issue in the slightest; in fact, it was actually the cover art that drew a significant amount of controversy. The Beatles had requested a jacket that was photographed by Robert Whitaker, a British photographer. "The scene depicted the Fab Four, with huge grins on their faces and wearing white butcher's smocks, covered in slabs of raw meat and mutilated dolls" (Burrows, 2012, p. 85). Now, the story of the conception of the album cover comes with many questions, as there isn't really a clear story about how this grotesque scene was conceived. That said, the running theory is that "the Beatles intended the image to protest Capitol Records "butchering" the presentation of their music" (Miller, 2014). The 'butchering' referenced here refers to the fact that:

> all of the Beatles' US albums up to this point had been scaled-down versions of their British counterparts, leaving spare tracks to make up new money-spinning albums. This hadn't bothered the

band in the past, but the most recent albums had been conceived as complete packages and, although they were powerless to prevent it happening, they [the Beatles] were becoming irked by Capitol's uninvited artistic interference (Burrow, 2012, p. 85).

Regardless of the purpose, the execution made it to a week before the album's planned release, when the public outcry about the cover reached Capitol's ears. Very few of the original covers actually made it to the public; the majority of the covers were replaced by a less offensive photo of the Beatles just before the release. Though it did make those few original covers worth a substantial amount - "an original copy of "Yesterday and Today," still in its shrink wrap, sold for $15,300 on eBay" (Miller, 2014) - the album ended up being the only Beatles record to lose money, due to the substantial cost of replacing the original covers at the last minute. According to Terry Burrows, that last-minute change cost Capitol records approximately $200,000 (2012, p. 85). He goes on to note that "the Beatles themselves were completely baffled by the controversy: the photograph had already been used extensively in the British press to promote "Paperback Writer" with no apparent reactions at all. It was clearly a transatlantic cultural quirk (Burrows, 2012, p. 85).

It seemed as though July of 1966 might provide the Beatles with some amount of reprieve from controversy, that month actually may have been the most controversial month in their touring days. The beginning of July saw the Beatles performing a series of concerts in the Phillipines, immediately after their concerts in Japan, where the Beatles were carefully protected: "a total of 35,000 security men were employed throughout their three-day stay" (Burrows, 2012, p. 86). This resulted in the Beatles being quarantined to their hotel room when they weren't performing, which inevitably left the Fab Four frustrated, particularly when they tried to see the city for themselves, but were swiftly returned to their room. In fact, this escape and John Lennon's later disappearance to see the city forced the police to threaten to abandon the Beatles entirely unless they smartened up and followed the rules (Burrows, 2012, p. 86).

The Philippines controversy was a result of a miscommunication - a miscommunication that severely impacted the Beatles' reputation in the Philippines, as well as cost them a fair amount of stress, exhaustion, and nearly injury. After arriving in the Philippines, the Beatles attended a private party and then retired to their rooms to rest, because they had shows planned for the following evening. Unfortunately:

> The Beatles were unaware that the promoter of the shows had promised that the group would first attend a breakfast reception with the First Lady – whose husband, Ferdinand Marcos, had been elected President the previous November – and top government officials, along with 300 of their children. Manager Brian Epstein had told the promoter that the group would not attend, as the Beatles wanted nothing to do with politics (Mastropolo, 2016).

And so, when people came to collect the Beatles and bring them to the reception, Brian Epstein told them that "they were all still sleeping and that under no circumstances could they be disturbed" (Burrows, 2012, p. 86). After speaking to Epstein, ""they were starting to bang on the door," said Paul McCartney. "'They will come! They must come!' But we were saying, 'Look, just lock the bloody door.' We were used to it: 'It's our day off.'"" (Mastropolo, 2016). In turn, without even knowing it, the Beatles had caused a large international incident. Though they were able to perform their shows that evening for more than 80,000 fans, the "the media had made them into the country's enemies. "It was 'BEATLES SNUB FIRST FAMILY' – that's how they decided to present it," Harrison remembered. "The whole place turned on us"" (Mastropolo, 2016). Not only that: the first lady herself made a television appearance saying that the Beatles had let her down, adding to the public uproar.

When it was time for the Beatles to leave the Philippines, then, they received a mountain of trouble. As Burrows notes, "all hell was let loose - their hotel and the British embassy were soon besieged by bomb threats, and the local promoter refused to pay them the receipts from the concerts" (2012, p. 86). Not only that: they no longer had police protection against the now-angry fans, so their trip to the airport with porters that refused to help load their gear was violent and terrifying. One of the road managers on the tour was beaten trying to get the Beatles onto the airplane (Mastropolo, 2016). McCartney remembers the event:

> "We got to the airport and our road managers had a lot of trouble trying to get the equipment in because the escalators had been turned off," McCartney said. "So we got there, and we got put into the transit lounge. And then we got pushed around from one corner of the lounge to another. And so they started knocking over our road managers and things, and everyone was falling all over the place" (McCartney, quoted in Mastropolo, 2016).

Once they arrived on the plane, they met with even more issues before they could actually leave. Between having to pay income tax on their concert that they hadn't been paid for before they could leave to holding up the plane because of documentation issues, by the time the Beatles finally could take off, the Beatles were "angry and exhausted, and wondering why they had to continue doing these tours" (Burrows, 2012, p. 87).

Yet even after the Philippines fiasco, controversy continued to plague the band; unfortunately, another controversy that led to violence, bomb threats, and even the public burning of Beatles memorabilia. It would appear that July of 1966 was ripe for miscommunication when it came to the Beatles, because this next controversy was in regards to comments made by John Lennon in an interview done by an old friend in London's *Evening Standard*. John remarked that "Chritianity will go. It will vanish and shrink. I needn't argue with that… we're more popular than Jesus now" (Lennon, quoted in Burrows, 2012, p. 87). While the British audiences took no issue with Lennon's comments, it was 6 months later that the comments made their way to America, where the remark caused a storm of anti-Beatles activity.

The US magazine that quoted Lennon's comments went national, and suddenly, just before the Beatles' American tour, churchgoers and religious groups across the country were rising up against the Fab Four: "radio station after radio station, especially in the Southern Bible Beltstates, banned the Beatles' music. Some even went further, organizing public burnings of Beatles records and magazines" (Burrows, 2012, p. 87). Of course, after the violence in the Philippines, and seeing how angry the American public was about these comments, "Epstein considered canceling the band's upcoming United States tour if it might put them in danger from angry audiences, even offering to cover the $1 million loss himself" (Matthias, n.d.). Yet though they were offered the option to cancel the performances, no venue they had booked even considered the option, so the tour went forward.

In advance of the tour, the Fab Four did a fair amount of press in an attempt to put the controversy to rest. The most popular topic of discussion was whether or not John Lennon would be willing to retract his comment publicly: "with a puzzled expression and as good a grace as he could muster under the circumstances, John apologized. Then, as quickly as the incident had flared up, the matter was more or less forgotten and the tour went ahead" (Burrows, 2012, p. 88). As good as forgotten isn't quite forgotten though: the Beatles did face some backlash during their tour even after Lennon's public apology.

Not only did city councils in Memphis try to have the concerts cancelled because they didn't want the Beatles in Memphis, the Klu Klux Klan (KKK)'s anger over Lennon's comments continued, plaguing the Beatles across their tour. On several occasions, the KKK picketed Beatles concerts, casting a shadow over the otherwise enjoyable concerts. Their presence, of course, made the Beatles extremely uneasy, especially considering that members of the KKK were continually threatening the concerts and the Beatles themselves (Runtagh, 2016). The tension in the air was so high that when a fan tossed a firecracker onto the stage, the Beatles thought someone was shooting at them (Gould, 2008). If the Beatles weren't exhausted with touring before, this tour really brought out all their frustrations and exhaustions with being on the road, followed by these controversies.

The Beatles played their final live concert on August 29th, 1966 at Candlestick Park in San Francisco. After everything that had happened, they were done with touring, and they were particularly annoyed that all the controversy around their tour and Lennon's comments had overshadowed their recent album release - *Revolver* - which they believed to be their best album yet. The critics agreed:

> *Revolver* [...] saw the true birth of the pop album as a coherent body of work, not just a selection of songs thrown together. While the world has long since revised its perception of pop music as an art form - at the time, few would have seriously regarded something as radical as Elvis Presley's Sun label recordings as art - *Revolver* was perhaps the first album by a pop group to be treated as a serious work of art. With *Revolver*, the Beatles paved the way for a whole new direction in pop music (Burrows, 2012, p. 88).

The band had reached a tipping point where they wanted to become more focused on their music and the art behind their music, and spend less time singing their voices hoarse in front of massive screaming crowds. The Beatles decided that it was time for them to get serious about their music, and to do that, they couldn't continue touring. Once the tour completed, the Fab Four took a three-month vacation to recover from the events of the year, and then reconvened at Abbey Road studio to begin a new era of Beatles music: *Sgt. Pepper's Lonely Hearts Club Band*.

Sgt. Pepper's Lonely Hearts Club Band is defined as a concept album, though the concept of the band itself is only demonstrated in the first track "Sgt. Pepper's Lonely Hearts Club Band/With A Little Help From My Friends" and the final track "Sgt. Pepper's Lonely Hearts Club Band (Reprise). Regardless, the guise of presenting the album under a different band name offered the Beatles a certain amount of artistic freedom, and the freedom from the expectations of Beatles fans, who were still holding onto the four young men from Liverpool in tight suits with mop top hair.

Success meant that the public expected the Beatles to deliver not only another artistic masterpiece but a prophetic statement. To relieve this pressure, Paul developed the personae of Sgt. Pepper and his musicians, a new identity that would allow the band more creative freedom. They had become self-conscious of the Beatles, but as the Lonely Hearts Club Band they would have nothing to live up to (Turner, 2015, p. 179).

The Beatles longed for the freedom of artistic creation: to be able to create without the confines of the Beatles image caging them in. When Paul was flying back from his three month holiday in advance of the new recording, he was thinking about how he had used a disguise during his holiday to go incognito - why couldn't the Beatles do the same? It would certainly permit them the freedom of creation that they were dreaming of. This line of thinking brought about the creation of Sgt. Pepper and his Lonely Hearts Club Band. But why Sgt. Pepper and his Lonely Hearts Club Band? Well, as with much of Beatles lore, the answer isn't entirely clear.

There are two clear theories as to where the idea for Sgt. Pepper emerged; the first, relating to that trip home upon which Paul decided he wanted to create alter-egos for the group. As the story goes, Paul and roadie Mel Evans - the same roadie who was beaten when the band escaped the Philippines - were on the same return flight, and started talking: "the name of the fictional band came from Mal innocently asking what the "S" and "P" stood for on the pots of their meal trays. When Paul identified them as "salt" and "pepper," this eventually led to "Sgt. Pepper" and the beginning of Paul's brainstorm" (Rybaczewski, n.d.). Alternatively, there is the ever-popular soft drink Dr. Pepper, which was particularly well-known in America, where the Beatles had just completed their final tour: it's possible that the name was born from thinking of the soft drink. Regardless of its history, it's certain that Sgt. Pepper has become a well-recognized figure in Beatles history.

Not only did the name emerge from thinking of alter-egos for the Beatles: the band name itself has an aspect of historical attention to it. Paul's idea was to "use a title that appealed to the late Sixties vogue for long and surreal band names - Jefferson Airplane, Quicksilver Messaging Service, Incredible String Band, Big Brother and the Holding Company" (Turner, 2015, p. 179). And so, Sgt. Pepper's Lonely Hearts Club Band was born. Then, Paul decided that Ringo should play the main singer of the band: Billy Shears. Billy Shears, of course, is the singer of the well-loved track "With A Little Help From My Friends," which immediately follows the track "Sgt. Pepper's Lonely Hearts Club Band."

Now, before we delve into the actual lyrics of the song and consider some of the implications therein, we have to look at one other defining aspect of both the song and the album: the album cover. After the Beatles recovered from their previous controversy with the cover of *Yesterday and Today*, one might think that they would stick to a less-controversial idea for an album cover. Alas, this is the Beatles we're talking about, and as we've learned, they were pushing the boundaries of what was acceptable, and one of the best ways to do so at the time was to question what was involved in what the record itself included: "[*Sgt. Pepper's Lonely Hearts Club Band*] was certainly one of the first gatefold sleeves, and also the first high-profile pop album to include the songs [sic] lyrics printed on the sleeve" (Burrows, 2012, p. 95). That wasn't the most interesting part of the album itself, though.

Paul had the idea that the cover for the album should show the Beatles surrounded by their heroes and inspirations. His bandmates loved the idea; the producers, not so much: "EMI hated the idea: to them an album sleeve was not considered to be much more than an advertisement, so anything that obscured their prime selling point - the Beatles, themselves - was viewed as a bad thing. Epstein was equally negative about the concept. The band, though, were adamant" (Burrows, 2012, p. 95). In the end, the band won out, and then one of Epstein's employees was tasked with requesting written permission from each of the figures the Beatles wanted to include on the cover for permission to include their photo. Though the four bandmates each selected a variety of figures, there were inevitably a few names that were kiboshed in advance. It will come unsurprising to most that the three figures that had not been included - Jesus Christ, Gandhi, and Adolf Hitler - were all selected by John Lennon. As Burrows notes, those names were "vetoed on grounds of poor taste. Some things would never change" (2012, p. 96). That being said, one of the three technically did make it into the photo. According to Sir Peter Blake, one of the artists working on the cover:

> "Hitler and Jesus were the controversial ones, and after what John said about Jesus we decided not to go ahead with him—but we did make up the image of Hitler," Blake told the Independent. "If you look at photographs of the outtakes, you can see the Hitler image in the studio. With the crowd behind there was an element of chance about who you can and cannot see, and we weren't quite sure who would be covered in the final shot. Hitler was in fact covered up behind the band" (Peter Blake, quoted in Cormier, 2017).

the Beatles themselves were wearing "specially commissioned uniforms, Paul having been talked out of his original plan to have the Beatles dressed as members of the Salvation Army" (Burrows, 2012, p. 96). That isn't the only curious tidbit about the album cover, however.

Reader, we have discussed the "Paul is Dead" conspiracy theory in our previous sections, and will do a full exploration of it when we look at "Glass Onion." This conspiracy theory makes a prominent return in this album cover, albeit completely coincidental on the part of the Beatles. These clues to Paul's death are said to run rampant throughout the songs on the album, including:

> In the song "Taxman," George Harrison gave his "advice for those who die," meaning Paul. [...] the Beatles had formed a "new" band featuring a fictional member named Billy Shears — supposedly the name of Paul's replacement. A Day in the Life [...]

had the lyrics "He blew his mind out in a car" and the recorded phrase "Paul is dead, miss him, miss him," which becomes evident only when the song is played backward. Lennon also mumbled, "I buried Paul" at the end of "Strawberry Fields Forever" (in interviews, Lennon said the phrase was actually "cranberry sauce" and denied the existence of any backward messages) (Time Magazine, n.d.).

That said, the most fascinating portion of the theory actually exists within some perceived clues on the album cover. First, let's discuss Paul McCartney's height, which surprisingly enough, is a controversial matter. Official sources cite McCartney, Lennon, and Harrison as having the same height during their peak Beatles years: 5'10". That said, on the album cover for Sgt. Pepper, McCartney is presented as being taller than all the other Beatles, by a noticeable margin. According to Paul is Dead conspiracists, this, as well as the hand above his head, symbolizing death, prove that the real McCartney died in a car crash in 1966. In addition, "if fans placed a mirror in front of the Sgt. Pepper album cover, the words Lonely Hearts on the drum logo could be read as "1 ONE 1 X HE DIE 1 ONE 1" (Time Magazine, n.d.). Does this mean anything? It depends on whether or not you think that post-1966 Paul McCartney is an imposter. Regardless, this exploration does make for quite a fascinating tale in regards to the Sgt. Pepper album cover.

Now that we've explored the necessary history to have context while exploring the lyrics of "Sgt. Pepper's Lonely Hearts Club Band," let's take some time to consider the lyrics of the song and how they connect to the Beatles and their desire to move forward in their musical careers. The first aspect of the song that we will be considering is actually the title of the song, and a finicky little grammatical choice that says a lot about how the Beatles felt about Sgt. Pepper and his Lonely Hearts Club Band: the presence and absence of an apostrophe.

The album name, as noted on the album cover, is *St. Peppers Lonely Hearts Club Band*. The song title is 'Sgt. Pepper's Lonely Hearts Club Band.' Now, this could, of course, be a simple oversight, but we would argue that with how much painstaking detail went into the cover of this album, that the lack of an apostrophe is more likely the result of a specific decision. As you likely know, reader, the purpose of an apostrophe is to demonstrate possession. In this case, 'Sgt. Pepper's Lonely Hearts Club Band' refers to the fact that the Lonely Hearts Club Band actually belongs to Sgt. Pepper, whereas 'Sgt. Peppers Lonely Hearts Club Band' has no reference to possession. Since Sgt. Pepper and the Lonely Hearts Club Band were both figments of the imagination, or aliases for the Beatles, it's entirely possible that the missing apostrophe is a reference to the whimsical, technically non-existent nature of the band. It's possible that the Beatles wanted to make a point about lead singers not 'owning' their bands, especially considering the Beatles never officially had a lead singer. It's also possible that the lack of an apostrophe was done for the fans, so they had one more clue to mull over - something that John Lennon loved putting into his songs, as we learned when we discussed "I am the Walrus." Or, as we mentioned, it's entirely possible that the artist who painted the drum simply missed the apostrophe and it's an actual genuine mistake. Regardless of the reasons, the absence of the apostrophe is a truly curious notion, and has never actually been explained by any of the Beatles or anyone involved in the cover art for *Sgt. Pepper's Lonely Hearts Club Band.*

The song itself is also worth looking at as a whole, particularly considering the history surrounding the album, which we discussed at the beginning of this section. This song's purpose is a live introduction to a live singer, though the Beatles had just recently given up live performances. This is a particularly curious dichotomy because, if we were to read deeper into the lyrics than just the surface, it makes us wonder why the Beatles chose this specific time to introduce their new band to a live audience with a song. We'll remember that the reason the Beatles wanted to use the cover of *Sgt. Pepper's Lonely Hearts Club Band* was because it provided them the opportunity to release something to the world that didn't have any Beatles-esque feelings or expectations associated with it. Perhaps this song is in memory of the good old concert days, where the Beatles enjoyed being in front of a crowd, something they mention a few times within the song. Maybe, as part of the 'concept album' they wanted to find a way to introduce Sgt. Pepper and his band as a distinct entity from the Beatles, and the best way to do it was to put Sgt. Pepper in front of a live audience. Either way, it's an interesting choice for the band to be performing live when the Beatles had just decided to move on from touring onto bigger and brighter things.

The line "they've been going in and out of style/but they're guaranteed to raise a smile" is likely a tongue-in-cheek reference to the catastrophe that had struck the Beatles in the past year - because in truth they had been in and out of style. Some people loved them, regardless of their perceived slights, and others burned their records and picketed their concerts. The remark about 'guaranteed to raise a smile' is quite true: no matter what the Beatles were up to, they were always managing to make the world - or most of it - smile. This line also ties back to their early days, where they were surrounded, in concert, by thousands of screaming girls, each one quite literally smiling from ear to ear. In becoming global sensations, it had become nigh expected of the band to put a smile on people's faces when they were talking about the Beatles or listening to their music. Though the Beatles would unquestionably go through more rough waters before their breakup, they were quite right in using this line to reference their own history as a band.

In a similar sense "so may I introduce to you/the act you've known for all these years" also relates back to their history, but also to what they thought would be their future. This is the line that really cements the concept that Sgt. Pepper's Lonely Hearts Club Band is an alias of the Beatles; by referencing 'the act you've known for all these years,' Sgt. Pepper is referencing the Beatles and the expectations they felt like they were drowning under. In essence, this line demonstrates a re-introduction of the Beatles to the world as a studio band, wherein they would produce new works in a way that the world had never seen before. The line also refers to the fact that the Beatles have no intention of continuing to be the band that they have always been: they are stepping into new roles as a studio band, and are planning bigger and more unique musical options than they had as a touring band.

Finally, the song ends with an introduction: Sgt. Pepper's Lonely Hearts Club Band's lead singer, Billy Shears, aka Ringo Starr. This introduction, and the fact that Ringo was taking the role of the lead singer, demonstrate yet another shift in the Beatles as fans moved into the album. Ringo hadn't taken too much of a leading role in the Beatles when it came to singing and songwriting thus far; the band's unquestioned leaders were Lennon and McCartney. The selection of Ringo as the main singer not only provided Ringo the opportunity to take his place in the spotlight, but also showed the way in which the band intended to branch out and provide more opportunities for Ringo and George to take the writing and singing spotlights. In addition, as we mentioned earlier, the Beatles didn't have a lead singer, so having one for Sgt. Pepper's Lonely Hearts Club Band provided another distinction between the two bands for fans to mull over.

Now, before we bring this section to a close, it's important to recognize that the disguise of Sgt. Pepper's Lonely Hearts Club Band wasn't utilized after the first two songs on the album, save for the reprise of the opening song at the end of the album. We've discussed how the intent was for the Beatles to feel a release from global expectations, yet they must have known - or guessed - that their album was going to be a massive hit, because the well-prepared aliases ended up working solely for the purpose of the cover image, the first two songs, and the final reprise. After the album was released, *Sgt. Pepper's Lonely Hearts Club Band* went on to make its mark in the history books, but that mark was as an individual album, and an album of the Beatles.

Sgt. Pepper's Lonely Hearts Club Band has a fascinating backstory, an interesting makeup, and some well-chosen lyrics, making it a perfect inclusion in our honourable mentions sections. Though the song itself doesn't tell a specific story, when we consider the background of Beatles history at that time, we can see a story emerge through the past; in addition, there are many individual stories that make up the album and the song to make it even more interesting. Though the concept of Sgt. Pepper and his Lonely Hearts Club Band died with the album and the song's reprise, we salute them and the Beatles for weaving such a fascinating concept story together for us. The concept itself may have fallen short of the true 'concept album' the Beatles intended, but Sgt. Pepper is amongst the ranks of the unforgettable times, moments, albums, and songs in Beatles history.

Helter Skelter

When I get to the bottom I go back to the top of the slide

Where I stop and I turn and I go for a ride

Till I get to the bottom and I see you again

Do, don't you want me to love you

I'm coming down fast but I'm miles above you

Tell me, tell me, tell me, come on tell me the answer

Well, you may be a lover but you ain't no dancer

Helter skelter, helter skelter

Helter skelter

Will you, won't you want me to make you

I'm coming down fast but don't let me break you

Tell me, tell me, tell me the answer

You may be a lover but you ain't no dancer

Look out

Helter skelter, helter skelter

Helter skelter

Look out, 'cause here she comes

When I get to the bottom I go back to the top of the slide

And I stop and I turn and I go for a ride

And I get to the bottom and I see you again, yeah, yeah

Well do you, don't you want me to make you

I'm coming down fast but don't let me break you

Tell me, tell me, tell me your answer

You may be a lover but you ain't no dancer

Look out

Helter skelter, helter skelter

Helter skelter

Look out, helter skelter

She's coming down fast

Yes, she is

Yes, she is

Coming down fast

'Helter Skelter' is a particularly well-known Beatles song, and is receiving an honourable mention for storytelling in this particular case because the most interesting story about the song isn't due to any action of the Beatles themselves. There are, however, two truly fascinating stories behind the song itself that the Beatles did intend, and we will explore these stories before delving into Charles Manson's interpretation of the song that let to his belief that "Helter Skelter" held information from the angels about a coming holocaust.

According to Steve Turner, "Helter Skelter" was born from Paul's challenge to himself after hearing reviews of a single put out by the Who. "I Can See for Miles" by the Who was a fascinating tune - interestingly enough, inspired by the increased studio techniques used by bands like the Beach Boys and the Beatles. The song was the Who's biggest single in the US, and was the only one to reach the top ten of the Billboard top 100. It was a heavily praised song:

> *Melody Maker* described it as a "marathon of epic swearing cymbals and cursing guitars (that) marks the return of the Who as a major freak-out force." Rival news weekly *NME* said it was "charged with dynamite" and presented "an ear-shattering wall of sound, with penetrating, rasping guitars, heavy-handed drumming and constant cymbal crashing" (Turner, 2015, p. 260).

McCartney felt that he wanted the Beatles to try a song like this: something loud and exciting that still held a strong set of lyrics. And so, 'Helter Skelter' was born. The phrase Helter Skelter has two different meanings - Merriam-Webster defines it as both "in undue haste, confusion, or disorder" and "British: a spiral slide around a tower at an amusement park" (2021). Of course, the song is centered around the spiral slide, but also engages with the other definition as it maintains the sound of controlled chaos throughout the recording. In fact, musicologist Everett Walter commented on the structure of the song thusly: "there is no dominant and little tonal function; organized noise is the brief" (1999).

Controlled chaos wasn't only present in the music and the song itself: it was also present in the studio during the recording. Chris Thomas, who took George Martin's production spot for this song, remembers that: "while Paul was doing his vocal, George Harrison had set fire to an ashtray and was running around the studio with it above his head, doing an Arthur Brown" (quoted in Lewisohn, 1988).

This wildness in the studio during the recording reflected something deeper than just the chaotic energy of 'Helter Skelter' - it also reflected the internal conflict between the members of the Beatles that was bubbling to the surface during this time. Interestingly, music critic Tim Riley considered the ways in which the bandmates' conflict reflected in their music, and in particular in this song. He posited that rather than reflecting the energy of the Who's song, 'Helter Skelter' sounded like something that Yoko Ono - Lennon's partner, and a significant cause of discomfort within the studio for other band members - would produce" (Riley, cited in Everett, 1999). He also discussed the way in which 'Helter Skelter' reflects a direct opposition to Lennon's song 'Everybody's Got Something to Hide Except Me and My Monkey:' "whereas Lennon submerges in scatalogical contradictions in his song, 'Helter Skelter' ignites a scathing, almost violent disorder" (Riley, 2002).

Though the song appears to tell a story about wild, uninhibited sex, McCartney later suggested to biographer Barry Miles that the song actually had a more serious focus that was lost in translation. According to McCartney, "I was using the symbol of a helter skelter as a ride from the top to the bottom - the rise and fall of the Roman Empire - and this was the fall, the demise, the going down" (McCartney, quoted in Miles, 1996). It was a fundamentally different type of song than McCartney typically wrote, but it ended up being a massive hit for the Beatles - though not at all for the reasons that the band was expecting.

Born November 12, 1934, was an individual who would come to be associated with the phrase helter-skelter as often if not more often than the Beatles. He claimed that the Beatles were four angels, destined to speak to him through their songs and provide him with instructions for his future actions. When asked to speak to his crimes - including multiple murders - in court, he said the only reason he acted was because the Beatles told him to: ""It's the Beatles, the music they're putting out," he told the district attorney who sent him to death row. "These kids listen to this music and pick up the message. It's subliminal"" (Manson, quoted in Grow, 2019).

Books upon books have been written on Manson, his strange connection to Beatles music, and the horrific events he put into motion. Our goal here is not to discuss every aspect of Manson and his life; instead, we will give a brief overview of his story, and then focus in on his interpretation of 'Helter Skelter' and how it resulted in a murderous bloodbath. This will give us a greater understanding of the song itself and one way in which its intentions were drastically and severely misinterpreted.

Charles Manson grew up in a life of abuse, abandonment, and crime. His history of being abused was reflected in his abuse of others around him, often in a violent sexual nature, as well as his preference towards petty crime. He was imprisoned for various crimes first in 1952, and then again in 1957 - the latter for three years, which began a ten year span of wild living, but also strategic learning. Manson was determined to learn about using religion, particularly Scientology, as a tool of control over the people, particularly women, around him. As Aja Ramano notes, "Charles Manson's cult philosophy was really a mix of predatory social engineering masquerading as religion and self-help — mainly culled from Scientology, with its abusive tactics, and Dale Carnegie's How To Win Friends and Influence People" (2019).

Now, Manson wasn't just in it to garner a following using his newfound skills - he had a bigger task in mind. At his core, Manson was a white supremacist and a racist: he believed that he was meant to begin the racial Armageddon between the whites and the blacks. As the University of Virginia explains, "[Manson] preached that the black man would rise up and start killing members of the white establishment and turn the cities into an inferno of racial revenge. The blacks would win this war, but would not be able to hang onto the power he seized because of innate inferiority" (2021). He believed that if the black community wouldn't start the Armageddon, that he would start it for them.

Manson was released from prison in 1967, into a newfound world of free love, peace, and counterculture lifestyle. Unfortunately, Manson was easily able to manipulate the goodwill of 'hippies' at the time, and convinced them to join his cult which he named the Family. "He traveled throughout California, approaching young women in San Francisco's Golden Gate Park as well as Los Angeles's Venice Beach, presenting himself as a religious figure and urging them to follow him by surrendering their identities to him completely" (Ramano, 2019). Within the cult, Manson flagrantly manipulated the truth to encourage his followers to engage in crime for him.

Now let's explore Manson's perceived connection to the Beatles. Manson believed that the Beatles were the four angels embodied in Revelation 9. Professor Douglas Linder explains Manson's thought process, saying that Revelation 9: "describes prophets as having "faces as the faces of men" but with "the hair of women"--an assumed reference to the long hair of the all-male English group. In Revelation 9, the four angels with "breastplates of fire"--electric guitars--"issued fire and brimstone"--song lyrics" (n.d.). With this understanding, then, Manson believed that the Beatles were speaking to him through their songs, particularly through the White Album. To Manson, 'Revolution 1' meant that the Beatles were encouraging a revolution, 'Blackbird' was encouraging the black community to revolt against the whites, and 'Revolution 9' meant that the black vs white revolution was impending.

> From the beginning, Charlie believed the Beatles' music carried an important message – to us," Manson Family member Paul Watkins wrote in his book, My Life With Charles Manson. "He said their album, The Magical Mystery Tour, expressed the essence of his own philosophy. Basically, Charlie's trip was to program us all to submit: to give up our egos, which, in a spiritual sense, is a lofty

aspiration. As rebels within a materialistic, decadent culture, we could dig it (Grow, 2019).

In addition, of course, Manson took a deep interest in the song 'Helter Skelter.' Because he wasn't British and had likely never realized the connection between the phrase and the slide, Manson immediately connected 'Helter Skelter' with the chaos of an impending race war. Manson then named the race war Helter Skelter after the song; "throughout the summer of 1969, Manson had been hinting to his followers that if black Americans didn't start Helter Skelter, the Family should help it along" (Romano, 2019). And so, when three of Manson's followers were arrested, and Manson flew into a rage, worried that they would implicate him in a murder he had committed months before, he decided to take action and begin the race war, both to fulfill his perceived destiny, and to remove police interest from his arrested followers.

Manson directed his followers to an address on Cielo Drive, an address that Manson had come to associate with everything he had lost in Hollywood. In his early days, Manson was a budding musician, but was never able to get into the Hollywood music industry. Even with the help of Beach Boy Dennis Wilson, who Manson had successfully manipulated into lending thousands of dollars and even rooms in his house for Family members and attempts at recording Manson's music, Manson still fell short. Terry Melcher, friend of Wilson and the man who eventually denied Manson's request to sign him to a record label, lived at the Ceilo Drive address, which was one reason that it became the inevitable target of Manson's rage. Melcher had moved out of the address in advance of Manson's attack, but it seemed that the house, not Melcher, had manifested Manson's failures, and so it was the house that he chose to attack.

Manson himself did not partake in the attack, but on August 8, 1969, four of his followers broke into 10500 Ceilo Drive and brutally murdered everyone inside. The victims were 26-year-old Abigail Foler, who was set to inherit the Foler Coffee fortune; 33-year-old Wojciech Frykowski, an actor and writer who was dating Foler; 18-year-old Steve Parent who visited the residence to try and sell the occupants a clock to help make some additional money for college and didn't make it out the gates before the Family arrived; 35-year-old Jay Sebring, a Korean Army veteran and men's hair stylist; and 26-year-old Sharon Tate, a fashion model and Golden Globe-nominated actress (Ramano, 2019). After killing the occupants of the house, the Family members took action to ensure the murders looked like they were committed by the Black community: "this was the full vision of "Helter Skelter," and the real reason Manson's followers tried to make their murders look like they were done by the Black Panthers: If black Americans refused to start a race war, Manson wanted to start it for them" (Ramano, 2019).

The evening after the first bloody attack, Manson sent his followers to another residence with the same instructions: kill everyone. This attack took the lives of Leno LaBianca, 44-year-old veteran and army sergeant, and his wife, 40-year-old Rosemary LaBianca, a self-made millionaire. Yet again, the Family attempted to make this attack look like it had been committed by the Black Panthers by writing "chilling phrases on walls in blood, including "Helter Skelter"" (Ramano, 2019). This time, however, Manson was actually present for the initial moments of the attack, but left the violence and murder to his followers (Ramano, 2019).

Years later, members of the Family still believe that it was the song 'Helter Skelter' that really solidified Manson's perceived connection to the Beatles. Member Brooks Poston said in an interview that Manson believed:

> Helter Skelter is coming down. the Beatles are telling it like it is." Watkins said this was around the time, too, that Manson began using the words "helter skelter" to describe an oncoming racial conflict, "and what it meant was the Negros were going to come down and rip the cities all apart. ... Before Helter Skelter came along, all Charlie cared about was orgies (Poston, quoted in Grow, 2019).

Manson and his followers that contributed to the horrific murders were all eventually sentenced to life in prison, but that didn't stop Manson from sharing his beliefs about the Beatles and their music to the courtroom:

> "['Helter Skelter'] means confusion, literally," Manson said in court. "It doesn't mean any war with anyone. It doesn't mean that some people are going to kill other people. … Helter Skelter is confusion. Confusion is coming down around you fast…. [sic] Is it a conspiracy that the music is telling the youth to rise up against the establishment because the establishment is rapidly destroying things?" he continued. "The music speaks to you every day, but you are too deaf, dumb and blind to even listen to the music…. [sic] It is not my conspiracy. It is not my music. I hear what it relates. It says 'Rise.' It says 'Kill.' Why blame it on me? I didn't write the music"" (Manson, quoted in Grow, 2019).

The Beatles themselves, of course, were chilled and disconcerted by the connections that Manson was drawing to their music. None of them really quite understood how Manson was reading between the lines in their music, but they were all disgusted with the way in which he had associated himself with their image and their music. George Harrison put it best: "It was upsetting to be associated with something so sleazy as Charles Manson" (Harrison, quoted in Grow, 2019). The song that had been born from a McCartney challenge to create something loud and exciting like the Who had done had, without any intention on the Beatles' part, become intrinsically connected to one of the most horrifying and upsetting cult movements in Hollywood history.

That's not to say, however, that the music community wasn't going to try and change that connection. 'Helter Skelter' is actually one of the Beatles' most covered songs, in part because of the music community's attempt to return the song to its original glory. ""This is a song Charles Manson stole from the Beatles," Bono said before U2's Rattle and Hum cover. "We're stealing it back"" (Bono, quoted in Grow, 2019). In fact, after the Beatles breakup, McCartney never played the song live on any of his tours until

2004, when it became expected for the song to be on the majority of his setlists, even to this day. It would appear that the song needed some time to lay dormant before being brought to life again, with less of a connection to the chilling events of the late 1960s.

Though 'Helter Skelter' was never intended to be one of the Beatles most well-known tunes, because of the ramblings of a psychotic murderer, the song became associated with a non-existent race war and some of the bloodiest events in Hollywood history. That said, the song's original intentions, whether they be a story about a helter-skelter slide or a desire for the Beatles to have a big, loud song, are the ones that we should be keeping first and foremost in our minds: connecting the music to its actual purpose. Though the phrase will inevitably continue to be associated with Manson and his Family, it's the best we can do to share that the original story of the song was about a slide and teenage sex, not race wars and murder.

Glass Onion

I told you about strawberry fields

You know the place where nothing is real

Well here's another place you can go

Where everything flows.

Looking through the bent-backed tulips

To see how the other half live

Looking through a glass onion.

I told you about the walrus and me, man

You know we're as close as can be, man

Well here's another clue for you all

The walrus was Paul.

The BEATLES

Standing on the cast iron shore, yeah

Lady Madonna trying to make ends meet, yeah

Looking through the glass onion

Oh yeah, oh yeah, oh yeah

Looking through the glass onion.

I told you about the fool on the hill

I tell you man he's living there still

Well here's another place you can be

Listen to me.

Fixing a hole in the ocean

Trying to make a dove-tail joint, yeah

Looking through a glass onion.

It's particularly fitting that "Glass Onion" is the final song that we consider in this book if for no reason but the fact that it is a teasing and entertaining summary of many popular Beatles tunes up until this point in their career. There's no question that "Glass Onion" is one of the less popular Beatles tunes, but it's also one of the most engaging because its self-reference leads to some incredibly fascinating history. Our exploration of "Glass Onion" will take us many places - deep into the 'McCartney is Dead' conspiracy theory, into Lennon's frustrations with the Beatles' perceived status as prophets, and into Lennon's unique response to fans who tended to take Beatles songs a little bit to seriously - and will provide us with a unique understanding of one of what we authors would argue is the most creative Beatles song yet.

Our analysis begins, as it logically should, with the reason behind the creation of the song. It's important to provide ourselves with some context here: "Glass Onion" was released on the White Album, for which most of the material was written while the Beatles were on their meditative retreat in India. They were long past their touring days, and their last album *The Magical Mystery Tour* had been the first Beatles album without Brian Epstein, which created a myriad of troubles for the band who was so used to having Epstien around for assistance. That said, this song emerged from the frustrations that Lennon had towards Beatles fans who felt that the Beatles were imbuing their songs with deeper meanings. As Steve Turner notes, "'Glass Onion' was a playful response by John to those who pored over his work looking for hidden meanings" (Turner, 2015, p. 234). Much like "I am the Walrus," there is a certain amount of entertainment provided by exploring a song that is intended to be confusing, but "Glass Onion" has additional layers when compared to "I am the Walrus" simply because of its intention, and reference to previous Beatles songs.

Now, when we discussed "I am the Walrus," we discussed Lennon's preference to creating convoluted and confusing images and verbiage purposefully intended to confuse those people (like the authors of this book) that seeked to find deeper meaning in Beatles songs. That said, we also explored the dichotomy of the fact that by creating songs that are intended to confuse, the songs inherently tell a story in themselves. We will be taking the same lens as we explore "Glass Onion," because even though this song is intended to poke fun at the people that explore the deeper meaning within Beatles songs, the song does create some interesting references to theories, ideas, and imagery that Beatles fans and fanatics alike had adopted in the 1960s, and whose legacies continue to exist today.

It makes sense, then, to explore the lyrics themselves to see what we can learn from their organization and contents. Lennon first makes reference to "Strawberry Fields Forever," by singing "I told you about Strawberry Fields/you know the place where nothing is real." The first three words in the song speak volumes about the song's intention, because by saying "I told you," Lennon is insinuating that there are deeper meanings within the previous Beatles songs that he'd denied those meanings existed in. "I told you" suggests that Lennon had told Beatles fans about specific aspects within Beatles songs in the past, which lends towards confirming the beliefs that Beatles fans had about the contents of Beatles songs. "I told you" is, in a way, an affirmation, which sets the tone for the song: teasing and playful to those who know its intent, and serious and focused to those who deem the song to be a truthful exploration of Beatles discography.

The concept of "looking through the bent-back tulips" is also curious, and is likely an attempt by Lennon at creating confusing imagery. At the same time, though, there is a perfectly reasonable explanation for that particular image. There was a particularly fancy restaurant in London in the 1960s known as the Parkes, which used an arrangement of tulips. As Derek Taylor, former Apple Press Officer noted:

> You'd be in Parkes sitting around your table wondering what's going on with the flowers and then you'd realize that they were actually tulips with their petals bent all the way back so you could see the reverse side of the petals and also the stamen. This is what John meant about 'seeing how the other half lives.' He meant seeing how the other half of the flower lives but also, because it

was an expensive restaurant, how the other half of society lived" (Derek Taylor, quoted in Steve Turner, 2015, p. 234).

It's references like these that really do make you wonder if Lennon thought he was creating these confusing and convoluted images that no one would be able to understand, or if he was purposefully including images that had reference to something in a song that was intended to reference nothing. In the latter sense, we authors have no doubt that Lennon had the final laugh when it came to the purpose and understanding of references like these, but did want to note the interesting dichotomy once more of finding meaning where none is supposed to exist. That said, it is also entirely possible that Lennon's image is nothing more than his imagination, and Beatles fans like Derek Taylor believed that they had found the answer when in truth, no answer exists. Unfortunately, we will never know the truth to these answers, which is a fact we must keep in our minds as we continue our exploration of "Glass Onion" and other Beatles tunes.

Now it's time for us to explore the concept of a glass onion, and why John likely selected that specific image to represent this concept of stories that had no meaning, or meanings that referenced stories he viewed as unrealistic and ridiculous. There are many thoughts in regards to exactly what a glass onion is, and we'll explore some of those theories now to come to a better conclusion of why this image headlined the intentions of this song. First, the more definite definitions. Originally, "glass onions were large hand blown glass bottles used aboard sailing ships to hold wine or brandy. For increased stability on rough seas, the bottles were fashioned with a wide-bottom shape to prevent toppling, thus making the bottles look somewhat onion-shaped" (Definitions.net, 2021). Is it likely that this is what Lennon was referencing when he coined the song? It's doubtful - based on the song's purpose, it makes more sense that Lennon was aiming for something based in imagination - but it is interesting to note that the term has an actual purpose outside of a Beatles-ism.

Beatles fans believed that a glass onion was a reference to a glass-topped coffin, feeding into the 'Paul is Dead' conspiracy theory that we will discuss in the next set of lyrics. The general understanding of a glass onion, though, is "something that would have layer after layer peeled away only to realize it was transparent after all" (Urban Dictionary, 2006). This logic follows John Lennon's in that no matter how many layers of understanding Beatles fans pull from Beatles tunes, they peel everything away only to realize that there was no meaning after all. That said, glass onion also references the way in which Lennon has put the song itself together: layer upon layer of meaning that actually means nothing. It's quite the ingenious image, because it is both logical and illogical at the same time: quintessentially Lennon.

The most referenced lyric from "Glass Onion," and the lyric that leads us to an exploration of the mythical "Paul is Dead" conspiracy theory is thus: "now here's another clue for you all/the walrus was Paul." Of course, to be able to truly understand this reference, and the irritation but also amusement with which Lennon viewed fans that believed the conspiracy theory, it's time for us to jump into one of the most convoluted and fascinating conspiracy theories of all time, which centres around a single question: is the Paul McCartney we see in the news today the actual James Paul McCartney?

The "Paul is Dead" conspiracy theory is one of the craziest conspiracy theories in rock'n'roll history, and that's saying something. The conspiracy began with a Detroit DJ fulfilling a request from an anonymous caller:

> [The conspiracy theory] blew up on October 12, 1969, when Russ Gibb was hosting his show on WKNR. A mysterious caller told him to put on the Beatles' White Album and spin the "number nine, number nine" intro from "Revolution 9" backwards. When Gibb tried it on the air, he heard the words, "Turn me on, dead man" (Sheffield, 2019).

From then on, the bizarre clues and fascinating theories just kept on coming. It would take a full book for us to explore all the details of the conspiracy theory, so we're going to take the time here to explore some of the most common and well-known aspects of the theory so that we can have a really clear understanding of why John Lennon made the reference he did in "Glass Onion." To begin, let's have a look at an overview of the conspiracy theory. According to theorists, James Paul McCartney was killed in a car crash on November 9, 1966. Instead of admitting his death, the rest of the Beatles decided to hire a McCartney lookalike so that they could continue with their Beatles fame and fortune.

The theory states that the rest of the Beatles felt remorse for covering up Paul's death, so they left specific clues within their songs and album covers for their fans to find and uncover. Now, with a conspiracy theory this wild, there's bound to be a ton of even crazier clues that match up to the theory, right? But of course! Let's dive into some of the wildest ones. To begin, let's look at the Sgt. Pepper album cover. Paul wears an OPD patch on his Sgt. Pepper uniform, which references the fact that he was 'officially pronounced dead.' Billy Shears was intended to act as Paul's replacement, since he couldn't be a part of the band because he was dead. "If fans placed a mirror in front of the Sgt. Pepper album cover, the words Lonely Hearts on the drum logo could be read as "1 ONE 1 X HE DIE 1 ONE 1"" (Time Magazine, n.d.). Not only that: if you play "I'm So Tired" backwards, you can hear Lennon say "Paul is dead, miss him, miss him," and at the end of "Strawberry Fields," Lennon also says "I buried Paul." Lennon, of course, has denied this and said that the phrase is actually 'cranberry sauce.'

"I am the Walrus" played a big part in the "Paul is Dead" conspiracy theory because "the black walrus symbolizes death in certain Scandinavian cultures, and McCartney was undoubtedly in that animal costume" (Chen, 2017). This concept entertained Lennon, who then elected to include the line "the walrus was Paul" in "Glass Onion." According to theorists, Lennon included this line to officially confirm McCartney's death. According to Lennon himself, the line was included to poke fun at the theorists, who he believed were completely out of their minds. Interestingly, "I am the Walrus" was also intended to poke fun at those Beatles fans that desired to find deeper meaning within Beatles songs, so the fact that Lennon was able to connect the two teasing songs together based on Beatles conspiracy theorist's ravings is particularly poignant.

The other big aspect of the "Paul is Dead" conspiracy is found in the Abbey Road album cover. On the surface, it looks as if it's just the Beatles crossing the street. To trained Beatles conspiracy theorists, however, the image represents definitive truth that their beloved McCartney is actually dead:

> In the picture, John is wearing all white, just like a priest; Ringo's all dressed in black like a pallbearer; and George is bringing up the rear in a blue-jean getup, the gravedigger of the group. And Paul? The supposedly deceased Beatle walks shoeless across the road, theorists say, because he's dead (Chen, 2017).

Not only is Paul shoeless in the image (because who needs shoes if they're dead?): he's also holding his cigarette in his right hand even though he is left-handed, and he's walking out of step with the other Beatles - further signs that he has moved on.

Of course, there are many other aspects to the "Paul is Dead" conspiracy, predominantly surrounding what happens if you play specific Beatles songs backwards and what you hear at that point, but from the above information, we have gained an understanding of what the conspiracy theory looks like, and why it's so fascinating, curious, and absolutely crazy. Rob Sheffield sums it up best: "the imposter wrote "Hey Jude" and "Blackbird," which means he's the guy who probably should have had Paul's job in the first place" (Sheffield, 2019).

Now, there's more to "Glass Onion" than just the "Paul is Dead" conspiracy theory, so let's continue to make our way through the remainder of the lyrics in the song to see what other curious notions we can glean from them. According to Steve Turner, the 'Cast Iron Shore' was nothing more than "Liverpool's own beach (also known as the "Cassie"), so-called because it was close to St. Michael's Church, Aigburth, built of cast iron by John Cragg of the Mersey Iron Foundry in 1815 and referred to locally as the Cast-Iron Church" (Turner, 2015, p. 234). Lennon then moves on to reference Lady Madonna, from the popular Beatles tune "Lady Madonna."

He returns to opening the final verse with "I told you," adding to the conspiracy theorists' interest in the song; as if Lennon is confessing to them. He speaks to the fool on the hill and fixing a hole in the ocean, two additional references to previous Beatles songs, before making a reference to a dovetail joint which is, in fact, "a wood joint using wedge-shaped tenons" (Turner, 2015, p. 234). The end of the song sneaks up on listeners fairly quickly - unlike many Beatles songs which feature gradual endings, this song simply ends once the lyrics are complete. Does this symbolize Lennon having no more confessions to make? Only Lennon and the conspiracy theorists know for sure.

"Glass Onion" is a particularly curious Beatles song because like "I am the Walrus," its intent is to poke fun at the people who work to find deeper meaning within Beatles songs. That said, in order to poke fun in the best way possible, Lennon created purposeful ties to older Beatles songs and conspiracy theories to better laugh at the ways in which Beatles fans would interpret the purposefully confusing tune. We can now smile happily knowing that, if Lennon is out there, he's having a good laugh at our expense as we took the time to explore the meaning behind a song built to exist without real meaning.

Conclusion: The Beatles and Storytelling

Storytelling is the basis of human existence. People connect by telling each other stories: stories about their day, stories about their lives, and wonderful stories they've dreamed up in their mind. Stories of love and heartbreak, success and failure, and fortune and famine are expressed in all languages, all cultures, and all across the world. These stories are told in a variety of ways: through the ages, oral storytelling and the tradition of passing stories down from generation to generation evolved to written stories, which has evolved further to digital storytelling through social and digital media. One thing has remained the same through all these years, though: stories are used to bring people together.

Stories with morals are used to teach young children lessons about the world they are eventually going to inherit. Stories about an individual's personal experience can impart unquestionable wisdom to those who listen. Stories about historical events make up our understanding of history and the worlds that came before us. Through the stories of eyewitnesses, we are able to, in some capacity, comprehend atrocities like world wars and genocides. Eyewitness stories can also recount beautiful moments like the way it felt to experience the Woodstock concert and the celebration of the end of the war. We see our world through stories: our stories, the stories of our peers, and the stories of the past make up the lens through which we see and understand the world around us, and the knowledge with which we navigate the world.

Music exists to tell stories in a new way. From the beginning of time, music was used to impart knowledge, share stories, and create connection.

Folk songs brought people together to sing, and to share stories. When they couldn't express their feelings in words, people turned to music to create feelings of immense sorrow, great joy, and everything in-between. Stories bring meaning to music; offering listeners new stories, new ways to think about the world around them, and new opportunities to experience their reality. Understanding the stories that songs are trying to tell us is an incredible experience, because it's easy to connect our lived experience with the music that we listen to. We connect to music that expresses the world in the ways that we understand. If we are in love, we listen to love songs and we connect those love songs to our own experience. If we recently experienced a breakup, whenever we listen to a song that relates to a breakup, we connect the stories in those songs to our own breakup story. We connect our memories to songs, and when we hear those songs, we are instantly taken back to the time when we heard them. The first song we heard at our wedding will have us slow-dancing around the kitchen. The song that played at our friend's funeral will bring tears to our eyes. At its core, music is storytelling: the telling of our stories and other stories to us and the people around us.

Music is universal storytelling. In her preface to this book, Catherine Mardon touched on the discussion, and in our introduction, we talked about how music is a universal language. Music transcends boundaries to connect deeply to each and every person that listens to it. Even if the words are in a language we don't understand, we are able to understand what the music is telling us: if it is a happy, sad, or lonely song, we can tell through the musical techniques utilized within the song. Even though there are thousands of different genres of music across the world and across the ages, we can listen to a song and discern its purpose fairly quickly. After we discern its purpose, it's easy for us to imbue that song with our own meaning: a time we felt the way the song is making us feel, a memory that the song brings to the forefront of our minds, or connecting the song to the moment we hear it in.

If the Beatles proved anything with their expansive and unprecedented career, it is the truth of music as a universal language. The Beatles played across the world to audiences who might not have understood the words they were singing, but who found themselves caught up in the excitement and the feeling that the songs provided them. The Beatles brought different cultures together; after all, as we learned, they played a really important part in making Indian music and culture popular in the United States after their trip to India. When the Beatles were in their early days, they were extremely popular in Germany, and even went so far as to translate some of their popular hits including "She Loves You" and "I Want To Hold Your Hard" into German for their loyal fans. The entire world loves the Beatles, and at the height of Beatlemania, no one was exempt from the love and wonder that the world felt for the four lads from Liverpool.

There is no question about it: the Beatles were one of the most influential bands, both of the 1960s, and of all time. Though the band was only together for eight glorious years, those years were chock full of adventure, mischief, mayhem, and some of the best and most recognized music in existence. The Fab Four have certainly made their mark on history together, and then again when they went their separate ways to create solo acts and new bands. The basis of this book exists from the idea that "in an age of rapid social change when old leaders were being deposed and old philosophies discarded, the Beatles were often regarded as prophets and every song was scrutinized for symbols, allusions, and messages" (Turner, 2015, p. 233). Much like we did in this book, hundreds of authors and thousands of Beatles fans have spent hours upon hours painstakingly analyzing Beatles songs to find the deeper meaning hidden within. Of course, within these pages, we were only able to analyze fifteen of the hundreds of Beatles songs in existence, meaning there are far more songs out there to explore.

With that in mind, dear readers, we encourage you to follow your curiosity and continue to explore the wonderful, weird, and wacky world that is the stories behind songs. Pick out your favourite song and do some research on the band, the song, and the stories that the band likes to tell with their songs. You will, unquestionably, learn something new through your research which will enable you to listen to that song with a new lens. Maybe the song you thought was a happy song actually has tragic undertones you had never noticed before. Perhaps the song is truly a song of joy as it was written during a difficult time and told the story of survival and success. You never know what you will find when you take the time to explore what a song really means and why the song was brought about in the first place.

This concept - learning about the meaning behind songs - can be applied across the board; not just to Beatles music. Every single song in existence resulted from something, and by finding out what that something is, you recognize the work that the artist put into creating the song, and you become more understanding about the world that artist exists in and the art that they provide. There is no shortage of fascinating stories behind music and art in this world, and we highly recommend that you take some time and explore the stories behind the music and art that mean the most to you: it will change the way you think about the art and music for the better.

Though we touched on this topic during our analysis of "I am the Walrus" and "Glass Onion," there's no better way to conclude a book on the Beatles and storytelling than remembering the ways in which John Lennon went out of his way to create songs that sounded deep and meaningful, but were actually intended to be about nothing. He created songs like "I am the Walrus" specifically to confound fans and send them searching for meaning that wasn't there. That said, to create a song without meaning is purposeful, which means there is a story behind why an individual would want to create a song without meaning. Even when the intention is for there to not be a story, a story exists. We can appreciate the irony in this fact, and use it to fuel our curiosity as we move forward to explore the meaning behind our favourite songs.

Works Cited:

BBC Bitesize (2021). The Beatles: Lucy in the Sky with Diamonds [article]. Retrieved from the BBC Bitesize website on July 17, 2021: https://www.bbc.co.uk/bitesize/guides/zffny4j/revision/5

Beatles Bible (2021). Maxwell's Silver Hammer [article]. Retrieved from the Beatles Bible website on July 2, 2021: https://www.beatlesbible.com/songs/maxwells-silver-hammer/

Bedford, C. (2009). Waiting for the Beatles: An Apple Scruff's Story. In M. Evans (Ed.), the Beatles: paperback writer: 40 years of classic writing (79-82). Plexus Publishing Limited. (Original work published 1984).

Beech, M. (2019). Beatles' Biggest Fans Revealed By 1.7 Billion Streams As 'Abbey Road' Climbs the Charts [article]. Retrieved from the Guardian website on July 2, 2021: https://www.forbes.com/sites/markbeech/2019/09/29/beatles-biggest-fans-revealed-by-17-billion-streams-as-abbey-road-climbs-charts/?sh=61259a8b2d95

Belshaw, J. (2016). Canadian History: Post-Confederation [book]. Retrieved from the E-Campus Ontario website on May 15, 2021: https://ecampusontario.pressbooks.pub/histpostconfederation/front-matter/about-the-book/

Best, P. (2009). Beatle! The Pete Best Story. In M. Evans (Ed.), the Beatles: paperback writer: 40 years of classic writing (40-50). Plexus Publishing Limited. (Original work published 1985).

Belz, C. (2009). The Story of Rock. In M. Evans (Ed.), the Beatles: paperback writer: 40 years of classic writing (227-233). Plexus Publishing Limited. (Original work published 1969).

Blake, J. (2004). All You Needed Was Love [essay]. In M. Evans (Ed.), the Beatles Literary Anthology. Plexus Publishing Limited. (Original work published 1981).

Burns, G. (2009) Beatles news: product line extensions and the rock canon. In K. Womack (Ed.), The Cambridge Companion to the Beatles (217-229). Cambridge: Cambridge University Press.

Burrows, T. (2012).the Beatles: It Was 50 Years Ago Today. London, UK: Carlton Books Limited.

Cambridge Dictionary (2021). Music [definition]. Retrieved from the Cambridge Dictionary website on May 5, 2021: https://dictionary. cambridge.org/dictionary/english/music

Campbell, D. (2020). Detective who busted John and Yoko lifts the lid on corrupt 1960s policing [article]. Retrieved from the Guardian website on June 27, 2021: https://www.theguardian.com/books/2020/oct/18/ norman-pilcher-detective-who-busted-john-and-yoko-grasses-up-1960s-coppers-beatles-rolling-stones

Chen, J. (2017). Paul McCartney is Dead: Music's Most WTF Conspiracy Theories, Explained [article]. Retrieved from the Rolling Stone website on July 18, 2021: https://www.rollingstone.com/music/music-news/ paul-mccartney-is-dead-musics-most-wtf-conspiracy-theories-explained-120340/

Chiu, D. (2021). the Beatles in India: 16 Things You Didn't Know [article]. Retrieved from the Rolling Stone website on July 11, 2021: https:// www.rollingstone.com/feature/the-beatles-in-india-16-things-you-didnt-know-203601/

Cleave, M. (1966, March 4). How Does a Beatle Live? John Lennon Lives Like This [interview]. *London Evening Standard*. Retrieved from the Beatles Interviews website on June 18, 2021: http://www.beatlesinterviews.org/ db1966.0304-beatles-john-lennon-were-more-popular-than-jesus-now-maureen-cleave.html

Collins, S. T. (2014). The Rise of 'Guardians of the Galaxy's Rocket Raccoon [article]. Retrieved from the Rolling Stone website on June 16, 2021: https://www.rollingstone.com/culture/culture-news/the-rise-of-guardians-of-the-galaxys-rocket-raccoon-205130/

Corlett, O. (2001). A Short History of Paperbacks [article]. Retrieved from the IOBA Standard website on May 8, 2021: https://www.ioba.org/standard/2001/12/a-short-history-of-paperbacks/#:~:text=In%20the%20English%2Dspeaking%20world,by%20a%20host%20of%20imitators.&text=Probably%20the%20first%20true%20mass,into%20being%20in%20the%201860s.

Cormier, R. (2017). 11 Facts about Sgt. Pepper's Lonely Hearts Club Band [article]. Retrieved from the Mental Floss website on May 30, 2021: https://www.mentalfloss.com/article/80939/11-facts-about-sgt-peppers-lonely-hearts-club-band

Cott, J. (2013). Days That I'll Remember: Spending Time with John Lennon and Yoko Ono. Doubleday.

Coughlin, K. (2018). Tone Colour [article]. Retrieved from the Fundamentals of Music website on June 13, 2021: http://www.fundamentalsofmusic.com/tone-color.html

Crossley-Holland, P. (2020). Rhythm [article]. Retrieved from the Encyclopaedia Britannica website on May 10, 2021: https://www.britannica.com/art/rhythm-music

Crystal, D. (2021). Language [article]. Retrieved from the Encyclopaedia Britannica website on June 13, 2021: https://www.britannica.com/topic/language

Dartmouth College (2005). Researchers find where musical memories are stored in the brain [article]. Retrieved from the phys org website on July 6, 2021: https://phys.org/news/2005-03-musical-memories-brain.html

Definitions.net (2021). Glass Onion [definition]. Retrieved from the Definitions.net website on July 11, 2021: https://www.definitions.net/definition/glass+onion

DeRiso, N. (2017). George Harrison gets deep on "Within You Without You" [article]. Retrieved from the Ultimate Classic Guitar website on July 11, 2021: https://ultimateclassicrock.com/beatles-within-you-without-you/

Dewe, M. (1998). The Skiffle Craze [book]. Planet Books.

Dictionary.com (2021). Blackbird [definition]. Retrieved from the Dictionary.com website on July 17, 2021: https://www.dictionary.com/browse/blackbird

Dowse, T. (2011). The Ultimate Helen Shapiro [book].

Durham University News (2016). Research Reveals Pain and Pleasure of Sad Music [article]. Retrieved from the University of Durham website on July 6, 2021: https://www.dur.ac.uk/news/newsitem/?itemno=28329

Eerola T. & Peltola H-R (2016) Memorable Experiences with Sad Music—Reasons, Reactions and Mechanisms of Three Types of Experiences. PLoS ONE 11(6): e0157444. https://doi.org/10.1371/journal.pone.0157444

Encyclopaedia Britannica (2019). Pitch [article]. Retrieved from the Encyclopaedia Britannica website on June 12, 2021: https://www.britannica.com/art/pitch-music

Encyclopaedia Britannica (2021). Ūd [definition]. Retrieved from the Encyclopaedia Britannica website on May 22, 2021: https://www.britannica.com/art/ud

Encyclopaedia Britannica (2021). Lute [definition]. Retrieved from the Encyclopaedia Britannica website on May 22, 2021: https://www.britannica.com/art/lute

Encyclopaedia Britannica. (2021). Musical Notation [article]. Retrieved from the Encyclopaedia Britannica website on June 13, 2021: https://www.britannica.com/art/musical-notation/Other-systems-of-notation#ref64565

Encyclopaedia Britannica (2021). Melody [article]. Retrieved from the Encyclopaedia Britannica website on June 2, 2021: https://www.britannica.com/art/melody#ref182053

Encyclopaedia Britannica (2021). Consonance and Dissonance [article]. Retrieved from the Encyclopaedia Britannica website on June 2, 2021: https://www.britannica.com/art/consonance-music

Epperson, G. (2020). Music. Retrieved from the Encyclopaedia Britannica website on May 5, 2021: https://www.britannica.com/art/music

Epstein, B. (2009). A Cellarful of Noise. In M. Evans (Ed.), the Beatles: paperback writer: 40 years of classic writing (37-39). Plexus Publishing Limited. (Original work published 1964).

European Union. (2019, February 13). The 'Swingin Sixties' -- a period of economic growth. Retrieved from the European Union website on July 5th, 2021: https://europa.eu/european-union/about-eu/history/1960-1969_en

Everett, W (1999). The Beatles as Musicians: Revolver Through the Anthology. New York, NY: Oxford University Press.

Ferguson, Y. & Sheldon, K. (2012). Trying to be Happier can really Work: Two Experimental Studies [research study]. Retrieved from the Taylor & Francis website on July 6, 2021: https://www.tandfonline.com/doi/abs/10.1080/17439760.2012.747000

Felton, D. & Dalton, D. (1970). Charles Manson: The Incredible Story of the Most Dangerous Man Alive [article]. Retrieved from the Rolling Stone website on June 16, 2021: https://www.rollingstone.com/culture/culture-news/charles-manson-the-incredible-story-of-the-most-dangerous-man-alive-85235/

Fraser, M. (2018). Down in the Hole: Outlaw Country and Outlaw Culture. Southern Culture, 24(3), 83-100. https://doi.org/10.1353/scu.2018.0034

Get Song BPM (2021). Maxwell's Silver Hammer [article]. Retrieved from the Get Song BPM website on July 3, 2021: https://getsongbpm.com/song/maxwell-s-silver-hammer/y8RMmV

Gibbs, J. (2011). An Agent Responds to 'Paperback Writer' by the Beatles [article]. Retrieved from the Nathan Bransford website on August 7, 2021: https://nathanbransford.com/blog/2011/08/agent-responds-to-paperback-writer-by

Giles, J. (2015). The X-Rated Reason John Lennon Called Eric Burdon the Eggman [article]. Retrieved from the Ultimate Classic Rock website on June 21, 2021: https://ultimateclassicrock.com/john-lennon-eric-burdon-eggman/

Gilmore, M. (2016). Beatles' Acid Test: How LSD Opened the Door to 'Revolver.' [article]. Retrieved from the Rolling Stone website on July 1, 2021: https://www.rollingstone.com/feature/beatles-acid-test-how-lsd-opened-the-door-to-revolver-251417/

Goodreads (2021). In His Own Write Quotes [page]. Retrieved from the Goodreads website on June 20, 2021: https://www.goodreads.com/work/quotes/1947892-in-his-own-write

Gould, J. (2008). Can't Buy Me Love: the Beatles, Britain and America. Piatkus

Green, R. L. (2021). Lewis Carroll [webpage]. Retrieved from the Encyclopaedia Britannica website on July 17, 2021: https://www.britannica.com/biography/Lewis-Carroll

Grow, K. (2019). Charles Manson: How Cult Leader's Twisted Beatles Obsession Inspired Family Murders [article]. Retrieved from the Rolling Stone website on May 23, 2021: https://www.rollingstone.com/feature/charles-manson-how-cult-leaders-twisted-beatles-obsession-inspired-family-murders-107176/

Harrison, G. (1967). Within You Without You [song]. Lyrics retrieved from the musixmatch website on July 21, 2021: https://www.musixmatch.com/lyrics/The-Beatles/Within-You-Without-You

Hishon, K. (2016). Exploring the Greek Chorus [article]. Retrieved from the TheatreFolk website on May 16, 2021: https://www.theatrefolk.com/blog/exploring-greek-chorus/#:~:text=The%20purpose%20of%20the%20Greek,going%20on%20in%20the%20performance.

Hoberg, M. (2017). The Different Types of Guitar Strings Explained [article]. Retrieved from the Gerank website on July 15, 2021: https://www.gearank.com/articles/guitar-string-types

James, E.T. (2020). The Beach Boys and the Beatles: How an international rivalry resulted in three of the most influential rock albums in history [article]. Retrieved from the Storius website on July 3, 2021: https://storiusmag.com/the-beach-boys-and-the-beatles-fb8647833dea

Jarry, A. (1996). The Exploits & Opinions of Dr. Faustroll, Pataphysician - A Neo-Scientific Novel [book]. Exact Change: Boston, USA.

Kerman, J. & Tomlinson, G. (2015). Listen (8th edition). W. W. Norton & Company Inc, New York: NY

Kim, M. (2015). The secret math behind feel-good music [article]. Retrieved from the Washington Post website on May 24, 2021: https://www.washingtonpost.com/news/to-your-health/wp/2015/10/30/the-mathematical-formula-behind-feel-good-songs/

Kreps, D. (2016). Paul McCartney Meets Women Who Inspired Beatles' "Blackbird" [article]. Retrieved from the Rolling Stone website on July 17, 2021: https://www.rollingstone.com/music/music-news/paul-mccartney-meets-women-who-inspired-beatles-blackbird-57076/

Lennon, J & McCartney, P. (1963). Misery [song]. Lyrics retrieved from Musixmatch on July 21, 2021: https://www.musixmatch.com/lyrics/The-Beatles/Misery

Lennon, J & McCartney, P. (1965). Norwegian Wood [song]. Lyrics retrieved from Musixmatch on July 21, 2021: https://www.musixmatch.com/lyrics/The-Beatles/Norwegian-Wood-This-Bird-Has-Flown

Lennon, J & McCartney, P. (1966). Paperback Writer [song]. Lyrics retrieved from Musixmatch on July 21, 2021: https://www.musixmatch.com/lyrics/The-Beatles/Paperback-Writer-2015-Stereo-Mix

Lennon, J & McCartney, P. (1967). Lucy in the Sky with Diamonds [song]. Lyrics retrieved from Musixmatch on July 21, 2021: https://www.musixmatch.com/lyrics/The-Beatles/Lucy-in-the-Sky-With-Diamonds

Lennon, J & McCartney, P. (1967). She's Leaving Home [song]. Lyrics retrieved from Musixmatch on July 21, 2021: https://www.musixmatch.com/lyrics/The-Beatles/She-s-Leaving-Home

Lennon, J & McCartney, P. (1968). Rocky Raccoon [song]. Lyrics retrieved from Musixmatch on July 21, 2021: https://www.musixmatch.com/lyrics/The-Beatles/Rocky-Raccoon

Lennon, J & McCartney, P. (1968). Blackbird [song]. Lyrics retrieved from Musixmatch on July 21, 2021: https://www.musixmatch.com/lyrics/The-Beatles/Blackbird

Lennon, J & McCartney, P. (1969). The Ballad of John and Yoko [song]. Lyrics retrieved from Musixmatch on July 21, 2021: https://www.musixmatch.com/lyrics/The-Beatles/The-Ballad-of-John-Yoko

Lennon, J & McCartney, P. (1967). I am the Walrus [song]. Lyrics retrieved from Lyrics.com on July 21, 2021: https://www.lyrics.com/lyric/267181/The+Beatles/I+Am+The+Walrus

Lennon, J & McCartney, P. (1969). The Continuing Story of Bungalow Bill [song]. Lyrics retrieved from Musixmatch on July 21, 2021: https://www.musixmatch.com/lyrics/The-Beatles/The-Continuing-Story-of-Bungalow-Bill

Lennon, J & McCartney, P. (1969). Maxwell's Silver Hammer [song]. Lyrics retrieved from Musixmatch on July 21, 2021: https://www.musixmatch.com/lyrics/The-Beatles/Maxwell-s-Silver-Hammer

Lennon, J & McCartney, P. (1967). Sgt. Pepper's Lonely Hearts Club Band [song]. Lyrics retrieved from Musixmatch on July 21, 2021: https://www.musixmatch.com/lyrics/The-Beatles/Sgt-Pepper-s-Lonely-Hearts-Club-Band

Lennon, J & McCartney, P. (1968). Helter Skelter [song]. Lyrics retrieved from Musixmatch on July 21, 2021: https://www.musixmatch.com/lyrics/The-Beatles/Helter-Skelter

Lennon, J & McCartney, P. (1968). Glass Onion [song]. Lyrics retrieved from Musixmatch on July 21, 2021: https://www.musixmatch.com/lyrics/The-Beatles/Glass-Onion

Leonard, C. (2014). Beatleness: How the Beatles and Their Fans Remade the World [book]. Arcade Publishing: New York, USA.

Lewisohn, M. (2005) [1988]. The Complete Beatles Recording Sessions: The Official Story of the Abbey Road Years 1962–1970. London: Bounty Books.

Lewisohn, M. (2009) High Times. In M. Evans (Ed.), the Beatles: paperback writer: 40 years of classic writing (132-134). Plexus Publishing Limited. (Original work published 2002).

Lewisohn, M. (2013). The Beatles: All These Years: Volume One -- Tune In. Crown Archetype

Linder, D. (n.d.). The Influence of the Beatles on Charles Manson [article]. Retrieved from the Famous Trials website on May 24, 2021: https://www.famous-trials.com/manson/244-influence#:~:text=One%20of%20the%20two%20great,the%20musical%20group%20the%20Beatles.&text=Manson%20believed%20that%20the%20Beatles,Album%2C%20released%20in%20December%201968.

Linguistic Society of America (2021). What is Linguistics [article]. Retrieved from the Linguistic Society of America website on June 13, 2021: https://www.linguisticsociety.org/what-linguistics

MacDonald, I. (2007). Revolution in the Head: the Beatles' Records and the Sixties (Third Revised ed.). Chicago, IL: Chicago Review Press.

Macurthur, T. (1968). McCartney's interview promoting the White Album on Radio Luxembourg [Interview Transcript]. Retrieved from: http://www.beatlesinterviews.org/db1968.1120.beatles.html

Madrigal, A. (2012). A Golden Age of Books? There Were Only 500 Real Bookstores in 1931 [article]. Retrieved from the Atlantic website on May 8, 2021: https://www.theatlantic.com/technology/archive/2012/06/a-golden-age-of-books-there-were-only-500-real-bookstores-in-1931/258309/

Marchese, D. (2016). Donovan on the Time He Helped Write a Beatles Classic and Then Watched John Lennon Chase a Paparazzo Into the Jungle [article]. Retrieved from the Vulture website on June 6, 2021: https://www.vulture.com/2016/11/donvan-on-helping-the-beatles-write-a-classic.html

Masterclass (2020). Guitar 101: What is a Bass Guitar? Learn About Different Types of Bass Guitars and 4 Tips for Playing Bass Guitar [article]. Retrieved from the Masterclass website on July 15, 2021: https://www.masterclass.com/articles/guitar-101-what-is-a-bass-guitar-learn-about-different-types-of-bass-guitars-and-4-tips-for-playing-bass-guitar

Mastropolo, F. (2016). When the Beatles Snubbed Philippines FIrst Lady Imelda Marcos [article]. Retrieved from the Ultimate Classic Rock website on May 30, 2021: https://ultimateclassicrock.com/beatles-imelda-marcos/

Matthias, M. (n.d.) Did the Beatles Really Say They Were More Popular than Jesus? [article]. Retrieved from the Encyclopaedia Britannica website on May 30, 2021: https://www.britannica.com/story/did-the-beatles-really-say-they-were-more-popular-than-jesus

Merriam-Webster (2021). Helter-Skelter [definition]. Retrieved from the Merriam-Webster website on August 23, 2021: https://www.merriam-webster.com/dictionary/helter-skelter

Merriam-Webster (2021). Music - definition. Retrieved from the Merriam-Webster website on May 5, 2021: https://www.merriam-webster.com/dictionary/music

Merriam-Webster (2021). Kithara [definition]. Retrieved from the Merriam-Webster website on June 14, 2021: https://www.merriam-webster.com/dictionary/kithara

Miles, B. (1997). Paul McCartney: many years from now. London, UK: Secker & Warburg.

Miller, M. (2014). The Beatles Cover that Generates Buzz, Bucks [article]. Retrieved from the LA Times website on May 30, 2021: https://www.latimes.com/socal/daily-pilot/entertainment/tn-cpt-et-0808-butcher-cover-beatles-sound-spectru-20140807-story.html

Museum of Patamechanics (2021). Apostrophe [article]. Retrieved from the Museum of Patamechanics website on July 2, 2021: https://www.museepata.org/tours

National Museum of African American History & Culture. (n.d.). The Little Rock Nine [article]. Retrieved from the National Museum of African American History & Culture website on July 17, 2021: https://nmaahc.si.edu/blog-post/little-rock-nine

O'Dair, M. (2014). Pataphysics: Your Favorite Cult Artist's Favorite Pseudoscience [article]. Retrieved from the Pitchfork website on July 2, 2021: https://pitchfork.com/features/article/9527-pataphysics-your-favorite-cult-artists-favorite-pseudoscience/

PBS (2005). The Sixties: Pop Culture [webpage]. Retrieved from the PBS website on July 5th, 2021: https://www.pbs.org/opb/thesixties/topics/culture/index.html

Pollack, A. (n.d.). Notes on I am the Walrus [webpage]. Retrieved from the Soundscapes website on June 20, 2021: https://www.icce.rug.nl/~soundscapes/DATABASES/AWP/iatw.shtml

Pollack, A. (n.d.). Notes on Rocky Raccoon [webpage]. Retrieved from the Soundscapes website on June 16, 2021: https://www.icce.rug.nl/~soundscapes/DATABASES/AWP/rr.shtml

Pollack, A. (n.d.). Notes on The Ballad of John and Yoko [webpage]. Retrieved from the Soundscapes website on June 20, 2021: https://www.icce.rug.nl/~soundscapes/DATABASES/AWP/tbojay.shtml

Price, C. G. (1997). Sources of American Styles in the Music of the Beatles. American Music, 15(2), 208-232. https://www.jstor.org/stable/3052732

Ramm, B. (2017). Why thousands of teens ran away from home in the 1960s [article]. Retrieved from the BBC website on May 15, 2021: https://www.bbc.com/culture/article/20170615-when-all-the-children-ran-away

Riley, Tim (2002) [1988]. Tell Me Why – the Beatles: Album by Album, Song by Song, the Sixties and After. Cambridge, MA: Da Capo Press.

Ritter, S. & Fergus, S. (2017). Happy creativity: Listening to happy music facilitates divergent thinking [research study]. Retrieved from the Plos One Journals website on July 11, 2021: https://journals.plos.org/plosone/article?id=10.1371/journal.pone.0182210#abstract0

Roberts, J. (2011). the Beatles: Music Revolutionaries. Twenty-First Century Books.

Romano, A. (2019). The Manson Family murders, and their complicated legacy, explained [article]. Retrieved from the Vox website on May 23, 2021: https://www.vox.com/2019/8/7/20695284/charles-manson-family-what-is-helter-skelter-explained

Rolling Stone (2020). 100 Greatest Beatles Songs [article]. Retrieved from the Rolling Stone website on June 6, 2021: https://www.rollingstone. com/music/music-lists/100-greatest-beatles-songs-154008/long-long-long-160188/

Runtagh, J. (2016). When John Lennon's 'More Popular Than Jesus' Controversy Turned Ugly [article]. Retrieved from the Rolling Stone website on May 30, 2021: https://www.rollingstone.com/feature/when-john-lennons-more-popular-than-jesus-controversy-turned-ugly-106430/

Runtagh, J. (2017). Beatles' 'Sgt. Pepper' at 50: Meet the Runaway Who Inspired 'She's Leaving Home' [article]. Retrieved from the Rolling Stone website on May 15, 2021: https://www.rollingstone.com/feature/beatles-sgt-pepper-at-50-meet-the-runaway-who-inspired-shes-leaving-home-124697/

Runtagh, J. (2017). Beatles' 'Sgt. Pepper' at 50: Remembering the Real 'Lucy in the Sky With Diamonds' [article]. Retrieved from the Rolling Stone website on July 17, 2021: https://www.rollingstone.com/music/music-features/beatles-sgt-pepper-at-50-remembering-the-real-lucy-in-the-sky-with-diamonds-121628/

Rybaczewski, D. (n.d.). Sgt. Pepper's Lonely Hearts Club Band History [article]. Retrieved from the Beatles Music History website on May 30, 2021: http://www.beatlesebooks.com/sgt-pepper-album

Sheff, D (2000). All We Are Saying: The Last Major Interview with John Lennon and Yoko Ono. New York, NY: St. Martin's Press.

Sheffield, R. (2019). 'Paul is Dead': The Bizarre Story of Music's Most Notorious Conspiracy Theory [article]. Retrieved from the Rolling Stone website on July 18, 2021: https://www.rollingstone.com/music/music-features/paul-mccartney-is-dead-conspiracy-897189/

Smeaton, B. & Wonfor, G. (Writer and Directors). (1995). The Beatles Anthology [Television Series]. London, England: EMI Records

Spitz, M. (2013). Rutlemania is back, and it's unreal [article]. Retrieved from the New York Times website on June 29, 2021: https://www.nytimes.com/2013/12/22/movies/homevideo/the-rutles-parody-the-beatles.html

Stark, S.D. (2005). Meet the Beatles: A Cultural History of the Band That Shook Youth, Gender, and the World. HarperCollins Publishers.

Sullivan, M. (1987). 'More Popular Than Jesus': the Beatles and the Religious Far Right. Popular Music, 6(3), 313-326. https://www.jstor.org/stable/853191

Sullivan, S. & Andreas, R. [eds] (2013). Remembering John Lennon [magazine]. New York, NY: Life Books.

Suttie, J. (2017). How Music Helps Us Be More Creative [article]. Retrieved from the Greater Good Magazine website on July 11, 2021: https://greatergood.berkeley.edu/article/item/how_music_helps_us_be_more_creative

The Associated Press (2009). Lucy Vodden, who inspired a Beatles song, dies at 46 [article]. Retrieved from the New York Times website on July 17, 2021: https://www.nytimes.com/2009/09/29/arts/music/29lucy.html

The College of 'Pataphysics (2021). What is the College of 'Pataphysics? [webpage]. Retrieved from the College of 'Pataphysics website on July 2, 2021: http://www.college-de-pataphysique.fr/presentation.html

The Winspear Centre (n.d.). Winspear Centre History [webpage]. Retrieved from the Winspear Centre website on July 11, 2021: https://www.winspearcentre.com/more/about/about-winspear/history/

Time Magazine (n.d.). Paul is Dead Conspiracy Theory [article]. Retrieved from the Time Magazine website on June 7, 2021: http://content.time.com/time/specials/packages/article/0,28804,1860871_1860876_1860997,00.html

Timmons, N. (2011). John, Paul, Jorge, and Ringo: Borges, Beatles, and the Metaphor of Celebrity Crucifixion. The Journal of Religion and Popular Culture, 23(3), 382-396. https://www.doi.org/10.3138/jrpc.23.3.382

Turner, S. (2005). A Hard Day's Write: The stories behind every Beatles song. London, UK: Carleton Books.

Turner, S. (2015). The Complete Beatles Songs: The stories behind every track written by the fab four. London, UK: Carleton Books.

University of Michigan (n.d.). Affective Musical Key Characteristics [article]. Retrieved from the University of Michigan website on May 24, 2021: https://wmich.edu/mus-theo/courses/keys.html

University of Virginia (2021). Helter Skelter: Charles Manson and the Family [article]. Retrieved from the University of Virginia website on May 24, 2021: http://people.virginia.edu/~sfr/enam481/groupd/helter_skelter.htm

Urban Dictionary (2006). Glass Onion [definition]. Retrieved from the Urban Dictionary website on July 11, 2021: https://www.urbandictionary.com/define.php?term=Glass%20Onion

Wardle, G. (2021). What Songs did George Harrison Write for the Beatles? [article]. Retrieved from the Far Out Magazine website on June 19, 2021: https://faroutmagazine.co.uk/what-songs-did-george-harrison-write-for-the-beatles/

Wiener, J. (2004). Sgt. Pepper and the Flower Power. In M. Evans (Ed.), the Beatles Literary Anthology. Plexus Publishing Limited. (Original work published 1984).

Wenner, J. S. (1971). John Lennon: The Rolling Stone Interview, Part One [article]. Retrieved from the Rolling Stone website on May 30th, 2021: https://www.rollingstone.com/music/music-news/john-lennon-the-rolling-stone-interview-part-one-160194/

Whatley, J. (2020). The Story Behind the Song: revisit 'Paperback Writer," the Beatles perfect ten [article]. Retrieved from the Far Out Magazine website on May 7, 2021: https://faroutmagazine.co.uk/the-beatles-paul-mccartney-paperback-writer-story-behind-the-song/

Woodhead, L. (2013). How the Beatles Rocked the Kremlin: The Untold Story of a Noisy Revolution. Bloomsbury USA.

Yamahaw. (2021). How a Guitar Makes Sound [article]. Retrieved from the Yamahaw website on July 15, 2021: https://www.yamaha.com/en/musical_instrument_guide/acoustic_guitar/mechanism/

Ze. (n.d.). Electric, Classical, and Acoustic Guitars: What Are The Differences? [article]. Retrieved from the Liberty Park Music website on July 15, 2021: https://www.libertyparkmusic.com/electric-classical-acoustic-guitars/

Zolten, J. (2009). The Beatles as recording artists. In K. Womack (Ed.), The Cambridge Companion to the Beatles (pp. 33-62). Cambridge: Cambridge University Press.

www.ingramcontent.com/pod-product-compliance
Lightning Source LLC
Chambersburg PA
CBHW031248090426
42742CB00007B/357